Unique
HANDMADE
BOOKS

Alisa Golden

Sterling Publishing Co., Inc.
New York

Library of Congress Cataloging-in-Publication Data

Golden, Alisa J.
    Unique handmade books / Alisa Golden.
        p. cm.
    Includes index.
    ISBN 0-8069-5813-8 Hardcover
    ISBN 1-4027-0614-6 Paperback
      1. Book design—Handbooks, manuals, etc. 2. Bookbinding—Handbooks,
manuals, etc.
    I. Title.

Z116.A3 G65 2001
686—dc21

                    2001034845

Designed by Wanda Kossak
Photographs by Sibila Savage unless otherwise indicated.
Art projects by the author unless otherwise indicated.

10 9 8 7 6 5 4 3 2 1

First paperback edition published in 2003 by
Sterling Publishing Company, Inc.
387 Park Avenue South, New York, N.Y. 10016
© 2001 by Alisa Golden
Distributed in Canada by Sterling Publishing
c/o Canadian Manda Group, One Atlantic Avenue, Suite 105
Toronto, Ontario, Canada M6K 3E7
Distributed in Great Britain by Chrysalis Books
64 Brewery Road, London, N7 9NT England
Distributed in Australia by Capricorn Link (Australia) Pty Ltd.
P.O. Box 704, Windsor, NSW 2756 Australia

Sterling ISBN 0-8069-5813-8 Hardcover
1-4027-0614-6 Paperback

CONTENTS

PREFACE

The paper waited expectantly. Inks peered through their bottles. Beads, ribbons and postage stamps looked up from my work table. "Pick me!" they all seemed to be shouting. I didn't know where to start. I needed to make forty new book art projects. I looked at the clock. I had an hour until it was time to pick my son up from preschool. I grabbed a big sheet of white paper and scribbled on it with pencil. I took out the inks and brushed them randomly on the paper. I played with paint and just let my hands start moving, trusting I would uncover a book. Eventually I wrote the text. After a couple of days, I discovered I had made the first new project of the forty that would become this book. I worked in this manner for several months, experimenting, playing, and trying not to throw something away before I had finished it. I made a lot of book art. I didn't like all of it.

Here I was, trying to write a how-to book for many other people, and I was working alone. I knew of book art that had already been made with structures similar to mine. I picked up the phone and began calling other bookmakers. At first I asked just a few people to send me some slides. Then I thought of a few more. Then some I really wanted to add. Suddenly I was corresponding with thirteen other people. This how-to book was evolving into something quite different from the book I had originally planned.

Left: *Flavors*, 2000; acrylic-painted, collaged, circle book in bowl made of acrylics, gel medium, and PVA; unique; 3" diameter
Right: Explorations from the 1980s

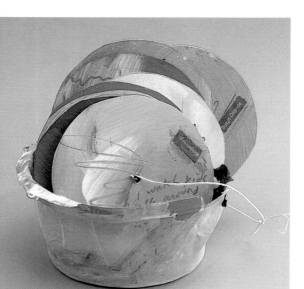

Wind Sends, 2000; leaves, acrylics, glassine; Jacob's ladder; unique; 11¼" × 5" (open)

By using techniques that some of these artists had used, I discovered materials and bindings I had previously rejected. I used them in new ways. I experimented with paper bags and wood and fabric. I found that I really liked cutting up old magazines.

But I wasn't satisfied just looking at the photographs of the book art. I wanted to know what the people behind the artwork were thinking when they made their projects. They sent me their statements, and I have included them in this book.

Everyone has a different approach. From fine press letterpress printed books to books made of honey and wax, each has something unique to say, told in a unique way by the person who made it.

Priority Mail, 2000; manila envelopes, glassine, stamps, hand-written text; unique; 10" × 7"

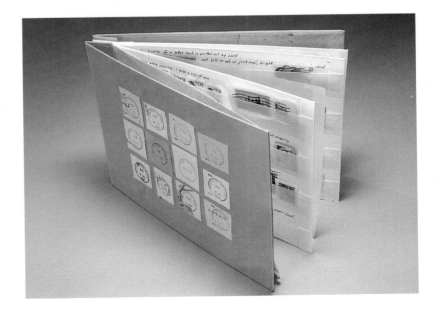

ACKNOWLEDGMENTS

I am fortunate to know many talented and creative people. I especially wish to thank those who contributed to this book, beginning with Betsy Davids, who was my teacher at California College of Arts and Crafts in Oakland. My connection with CCAC led me to Val Simonetti, Anne Hicks Siberell, and Anne Stevens. Upon graduating in 1985 with a degree in print-making but a passion for bookmaking, I joined the Pacific Center for the Book Arts, where I met Marie Dern, past president, and Alastair Johnston, editor of the organization's journal, *The Ampersand*. Through PCBA I was introduced to the work of Sas Colby, Katherine Ng, Robbin Ami Silverberg, Lisa Kokin, Julie Chen, and Coriander Reisbord, who is the current president. Lisa Kokin invited me to teach with her more than once at homeless shelters in Oakland and Berkeley. *Creating Handmade Books* tells about those experiences. I bought Catherine Michaelis's *Book: A Cherokee Primer* on a trip to New Mexico and wrote to her afterward. Years later she invited me to be one of 22 participants in the collaborative project *Stack the Deck* (along with Katherine Ng, Julie Chen, and others).

I also want to thank Nan's art and writing salon group, which tested the first rotating notebook project: Patricia Behning, Lynne Knight, Marc Pandone, Val Simonetti, Nan Wishner, and Yoko Yoshikawa.

Many thanks to my husband, Michael, whose loving, blunt honesty helped me revise the book before it went to the publisher. And to my children, Mollie and Ezra, who continue to inspire me.

Top: Catherine Michaelis (et al): *Stack the Deck*, 1999; 5" x 7 1/4"
Bottom: *Guide from Thin Air*, by Marc Pandone, page by Marc Pandone, 2000; rotating notebook project; 6" x 7 1/2"

Left: Robbin Ami Silverberg: *After Midnight*, by Ted Kooser, 1992; concertina fold-out, pulp-painted rag and iris-leaf papers, magnet, laser-printed text hidden in the folds of a night garden; series of 3; 13" x 15" x 7 1/2" (photo by R. Silverberg)
Right: Sas Colby: *Books to Read and Write*, 1992; acrylic on canvas, applied canvas letters, French-door format; 18" x 14" (detail); unique (photo by S. Colby)

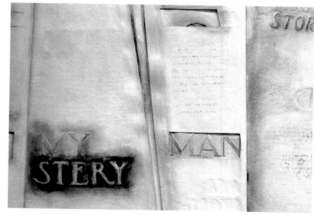

INTRODUCTION

Think of your audience when you create a book. Give the book a concept and put into the book only what is relevant to that concept. The book you would make for your great-aunt might be very different from the one you would create for your best friend. You would design each differently, depending on their favorite colors, things they collect, favorite fabrics or animals.

Your first books may be for yourself. Katherine Ng, a Los Angeles book artist and teacher, suggests that what you carry tells about your identity; look in your purse or backpack, bag or briefcase, then photocopy or scan some items. Or pick one item that seems suddenly interesting and work with it. If you don't know what to choose, put your hand in and pick something at random. Play with the shape, color, and content of what you picked. Start writing about your life; you must have some anecdote or story you want to develop and even share.

The bindings explained and depicted in this book are generally adapted from other structures. While they are meant to be intriguing, they are not an end in themselves. Each should give you a theme to get you started. Choose one structure and focus on that theme. Then add words or a sequence of pictures to give purpose to the structure.

To learn each binding, read through the instructions. Then read through them again and make a model. You can treat this model as a scrapbook and add content later, or you can make the pages of your book first. Design all the pages, then see if you are ready to bind them. By creating the pages first, you have the freedom to begin again.

Use your materials to strengthen your concept. Remember your audience. Play with the materials and have fun. You can learn how to design book art, add content, incorporate recycled materials, and work with other people to make a playful and meaningful book.

Don't Bother That Man, 1990; collage, photocopies, rubber stamps, typing, preparation for an edition; 5¹/₂" x 8¹/₂"

TOOL BOX

art knife and spare blades	PVA glue	pencil
cutting mat	wheat paste	³/₁₆" metal spacing bar
corrugated cardboard	glue stick	heavy book or weight
pencil	self-adhesive linen tape	drill or bit and brace
white plastic eraser	plastic containers	saw
ruler	paper plates	iron and ironing board
centering ruler	Masonite boards, smooth on both sides	seam binding
bone folder		straight pins
awl	stencil brush	quilt batting or craft and fabric fleece
needles	spray bottle	
threads and ribbons	mulberry paper	sewing machine
beeswax	waxed paper	iron-on transfer paper
scissors	magazines for scrap paper	fabric markers, paints, crayons

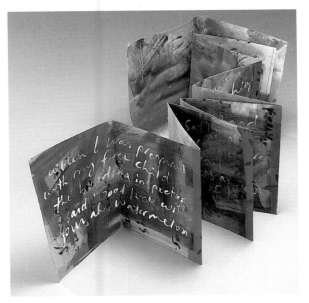

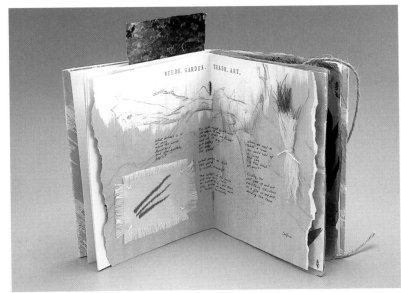

Left: *Watermelon,* 1998; acrylics, canvas, paper, linen tape; 7¹/₂ x 10¹/₂"
Right: *Loose Edges,* by Lynne Knight, page by Alisa Golden, 2000; rotating notebook project; 6" x 7¹/₂"

KEY TO DIAGRAMS

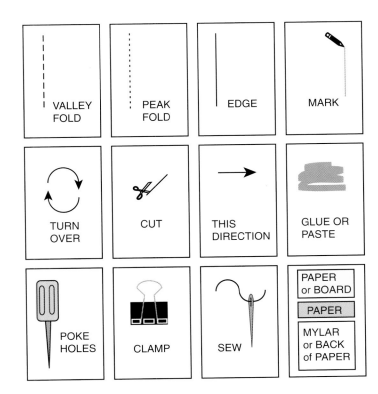

VALLEY FOLD	PEAK FOLD	EDGE	MARK
TURN OVER	CUT	THIS DIRECTION	GLUE OR PASTE
POKE HOLES	CLAMP	SEW	PAPER or BOARD / PAPER / MYLAR or BACK of PAPER

CHAPTER 1

SHAPED AND THEMED BOOKS

The physical shape of the book gives the reader a hint of what is inside. The following structures have specific shapes or themes built into them and should provide a good place to start. Use the shape of the book to give you an idea for the theme. Or take your theme and find a book structure that suits it. Katherine Ng used a trapezoidal shape for her book *Banana Yellow*, which examines Chinese-American culture. She chose a shape to remind the reader of a Chinese take-out box.

Katherine Ng: *Banana Yellow*, 1991; letterpress printed, recycled wire; 5$^{1}/_{8}$" x 5$^{3}/_{4}$" (photo by K. Ng)

"My artist books are inspired by the culture around me. *Banana Yellow* is a collection of anecdotes about my growing up in a Chinese-American family. The format of *Banana Yellow* was inspired by *Ordinary Wisdom*, a book of poetry by a poet whom I admire, Eloise Klein Healy. In her book, she wrote poems based on Chinese type that she saw in the window of a shop in a small town. She left a note saying that she was interested in some of the type. When she received the type in the mail, she had a friend translate the characters. Each word was the basis of a poem. In my case, I chose the words that I wanted to emphasize in my book and had my mother translate the words into Chinese characters. I rewrote the characters, then had them made into photoengravings, which I printed.

"The book reads like a set of bound flash cards where the pages turn from bottom to top. On one page, the reader learns a Chinese word, its Cantonese Romanization, and the English translation. On the opposite page, there is a short anecdote about the word. The title is a play on words where 'banana' is used in a derogatory way to describe someone who looks Asian but acts like a white person: yellow on the outside, white on the inside. (Yellow is the skin color designated to the Asian culture.)

"The structure of *Banana Yellow* reflects a stereotypical icon of the Chinese-American culture: the Chinese take-out box. I bound the books with original wire from these take-out boxes collected from many Sunday-evening dinners with my parents at a favorite Chinese restaurant.

"In *Banana Yellow*, I wanted to introduce the reader to a sense of my Chinese culture. Asian Americans have told me that they could empathize with my book, while others have informed me that they learned a new perspective of Asian-American culture."

KATHERINE NG

Ox-Plow Pamphlet, 2000; paste papers, collage, altered and found text; unique; 3" x 4"

OX-PLOW PAMPHLET
(FOLDING, SLITTING)

I have borrowed the form of the ox-plow pamphlet from a more elaborate form that Scott McCarney named *boustrophedon* (Greek for "as the ox plows" or "as the ox turns"). *Boustrophedon* is an ancient method of writing; if the first line was read left to right, the next line was read right to left, alternating back and forth. The back-and-forth nature of the folded pages is reminiscent of that writing. I have also seen longer versions of the structure with more folds and turns, sometimes called maze books. The short version works well as a flyer or pamphlet.

Tools: metal-edged ruler and art knife, cutting mat, bone folder
Materials: 1 sheet of 8^1/$_2$" x 11" medium weight paper

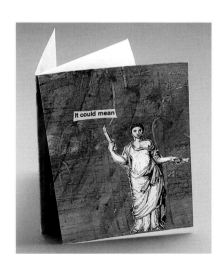

Ox-Plow Pamphlet, detail

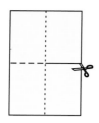

steps 1–6

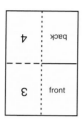

layout (front)

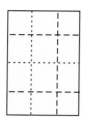

layout (back)

1. Place paper in front of you vertically.
2. Fold in half lengthwise. Open.
3. Turn it over.
4. Fold paper in half widthwise. Open.
5. You will now have two folds, one is a peak, one is a valley. Position the paper so that the valley fold is the widthwise fold.
6. Make a horizontal slit from the intersection of the two folds to the right edge. (Don't cut the paper completely in half!)
7. Fold the book according to the peak and valley folds.

OX-PLOW QUILT BOOK
(FOLDING, SLITTING)

The beauty of this book is that it is made from a single sheet of paper. Beth Herrick, Val Simonetti, and I used it to make *Betsy's Almanac* for our friend and teacher Betsy Davids for her birthday. Since her birthday is July Fourth, we chose texts about Betsy Ross, the American flag, the Statue of Liberty, and the holiday celebration itself. Four texts in red ink run concurrently across the pages like stripes. If you unfold the book you can see that there are 13 lines for 13 stripes. The back has collages (like quilted squares) around the edges. Under the collage on the back page (which becomes the back cover) we glued a ribbon so we can tie the book closed.

Katherine Ng glued some of the folds together in her book *Alphabetical Afflictions*, which makes it more like a typical accordion-style book, and not quite so springy.

Betsy's Almanac (with Val Simonetti and Beth Herrick), 1999; letter-press on handmade paper, photoengravings, ribbon; edition of 20; 2¹/₂" x 2¹/₂" (photo by Jim Hair)

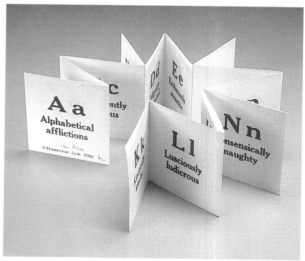

Katherine Ng: *Alphabetical Afflictions*, 2000; 2³/₄" x 2³/₄"

Tools: scissors, pencil, ruler, bone folder (optional)
Materials: one sheet of $7^1/2$" x 10" paper to make a $2^1/2$" x $2^1/2$" book

1. Place the paper in front of you vertically.
2. Fold paper in half widthwise. Open.
3. Turn the paper over so the widthwise fold becomes a peak.
4. Fold the bottom half up to the middle; fold the top half down to the middle. Open. You have four sections.
5. With the paper still vertical, make a mark $2^1/2$" from the left edge.
6. Bring the right edge over and align it with the mark. Crease.
7. Turn the paper over. The lengthwise fold should be toward the left.
8. Now bring the right edge to the lengthwise fold. Crease. Open. You should now have accordion folds that make a total of twelve equal-sized sections.
9. Put the paper in front of you vertically. Take your scissors and cut up along the left lengthwise fold for three rows of squares.
10. Rotate your paper so the cut is now coming down from the top right.
11. Again cut up along the lengthwise fold (which is now on the left). Leave the fourth row intact. Your paper should look like an "N".
12. Start folding up your paper, alternating valleys and peaks. When you get to the fourth row, your book will flip over and come back down the next row.
13. Your book should fold up into a neat $2^1/2$" square.
14. To add a ribbon tie: turn the book over so the back page/cover is facing you. Measure $1^1/4$" from one top and one side edge to find the center. Mark it with a pencil. Take a tiny bit of PVA glue and make about a 1" horizontal line. Find the center of your ribbon and press it on top of the glue line. Spread glue thinly but completely on the back of a $1^1/2$" square piece of paper. Press the square on top of the ribbon, centered on the back page/cover. Open the book completely and press it, sandwiched between waxed paper, under Masonite boards with a heavy weight on top.

steps 1–8

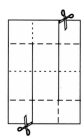

steps 9–11

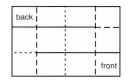

9	10	11	12
8	ㄥ	9	S
1	2	3	4

layout (front)

back		
		front

layout (back)

BRUSH BOOK
(FOLDING)

I got the idea for this structure from the "gum wrapper chains" I made as a kid. This little book uses the same sort of fold for the spine piece. The pages slip right in. I made *I Am the Groom* from newspapers: the word "rage" happened to appear on the spine piece and by good luck the word was appropriate to my piece. I stenciled rectangles of gesso onto the pages; for the text I used rubber stamps. If I had wanted my book to be archival or if I had wanted to make multiple copies, I would have photocopied sheets of newspaper onto all-cotton paper before I cut up the strips.

step 1

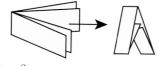

steps 2 and 3

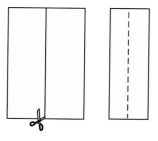

step 4   **step 5**

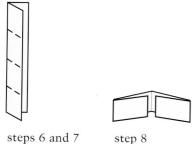

steps 6 and 7   **step 8**

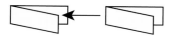

step 9

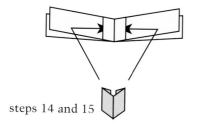

steps 14 and 15

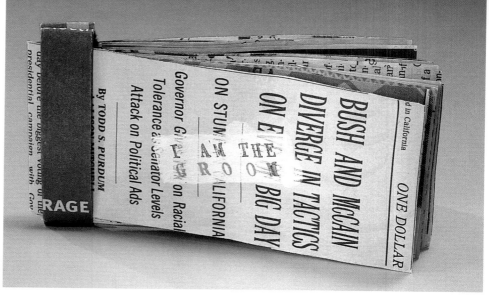

I Am the Groom, 2000; newspaper, gesso, rubber-stamped text; unique; 4¹/2" x 2¹/4"

Tools: scissors or knife and cutting mat, metal ruler, glue stick (optional)
Materials: Four sheets of 8¹/2" x 11" lightweight paper or twelve paper strips 2" x 11" and one strip 4" x 11", and one square of paper 2" x 2" (if paper is pre-cut, skip to step 3)

1. Cut three pieces of paper lengthwise into four strips each (making twelve strips total). You may divide the paper by folding it in half lengthwise, then folding the ends in to the center fold, or by measuring it with a ruler.
2. Fold each strip in half widthwise.
3. Nest the twelve strips, one inside the other.
4. Take the fourth sheet of paper and cut it in half lengthwise.
5. Fold one of the new strips in half lengthwise.
6. Keeping the strip folded, fold in half widthwise. Open.
7. Fold the ends in to the middle fold.
8. Fold back in half widthwise.
9. Slip the twelve nested strips into the holes created by the single folded spine strip.
10. Bend the pages toward the front and back of the book.
11. Take a square of paper that is the same height as your book (2") and fold it in half (folded with the grain, if possible). Open.
12. Fold the ends in to the middle fold.
13. Optional: apply glue stick to the two flaps you see now.
14. Open your book to the very center. The pages naturally split here.
15. The new folded piece will look like a "V". Tuck this piece into the interior slits created by the spine piece. The open side with two folded edges should fit in easily. The side with one folded edge (the point of the "V") will be slightly exposed inside the book.

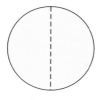

BOX OF CIRCLES
(FOLDING, GLUING)

For a circle book, cut circle shapes out of heavy paper, then poke holes in the middle, and thread the circles onto a thick thread or ribbon. With twelve circles, one representing each month, this would be a good structure for a list of birthdays. There are some things that never end: the cycle of the seasons, merry-go-rounds, paying bills. In his book *Structure of the Visual Book*, Keith Smith points out that a title page somewhere in a circular book inevitably gives the book a beginning, even if the contents can keep going around.

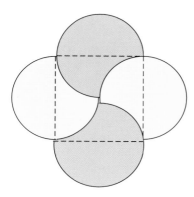

step 1

steps 2 and 3

Put the title of your book on the circle box and omit the title page for a completely circular presentation. I adapted the idea for a box of circles from a circle envelope in *Gift Wrapping: Creative Ideas from Japan*, by Kunio Ekiguchi. The box will hold a thicker book than the envelope.

Tools: glue or glue stick, pencil, ruler
Materials: four circles (use two of one color and two of another to emphasize the pattern)

To make an envelope:
 1. Fold circles in half. Open.
 2. Arrange the circles so that the valley folds make a square, overlapping in sequence. Glue down the edges. When you reach the last circle, glue it under one circle and over another.
 3. With valley folds up, fold over the flaps of each circle. When you reach the fourth circle, tuck it into the first one.

Nan's Birthday Book, 1998; acrylic-painted paper, handwritten text; 2" diameter

Birthday Book in *a Box of Circles,* 2000; unique; 41/2" diameter book, 43/4" square box

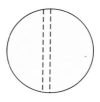

steps 1 and 2

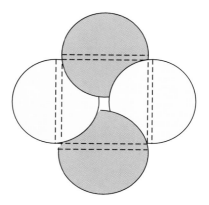

steps 3 and 4

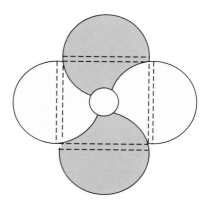

step 5

To make a box:

1. Fold four equal-sized circles in half.
2. Measure $1/8"$ ($1/4"$ for a thicker book) from the fold and fold the circles again. Each circle will now have a centerfold and an off-centerfold, making a shorter flap and a longer flap.
3. Arrange the folded circles with the off-centerfolds (the shorter flap) to make the square. There will be a small space in the center.
4. Glue down one circle at a time in rotation, as for the envelope (page 17), steps 2 and 3.
5. Glue a very small circle inside the box, over the hole in the middle.

DOUBLE SCROLL

The double scroll is an ancient form that can be seen in synagogues today in the Torah scrolls, the handwritten Five Books of Moses. The Torah is made of parchment and has many sections sewn together. You can make this scroll any length just by joining more paper. Glue will make the paper bulge when it is rolled. Glue stick may work but be a little stiff. Sewing will work best, and the stitching adds color and another design element to the completed piece. Purchase dowels in an art supply or hardware store, and saw them to the desired length. For added color, use paste papers for your inner paper. Paint

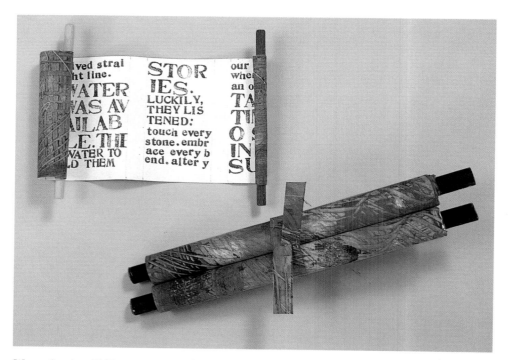

Water Stories, 2000; paste paper, dowels, acrylic paints, rubber stamps; unique; 5" x 1¹/₂".
Scroll Model, 2000; paste paper, dowels; 10" x 2"

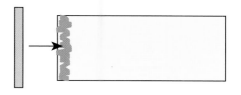

step 1

steps 2, 3, and 4

complete

gesso on the back of the paste paper first so the paper doesn't curl. Let it dry before proceeding. When you need to apply the glue, put it on the gesso side of the paper.

Tools: saw for cutting dowels, sandpaper to sand the rough edges, PVA glue, glue brush, magazines for scrap paper

Materials: Two wooden dowels (cut one long one down if necessary), light-weight paper for inner paper (cut 2" shorter in height than the dowels and as long as you like), book cloth or heavy paper for cover

1. Brush about a 1" flat line of PVA glue along the left edge of the light-weight paper.
2. Place the dowel on top of the leftmost edge of the paper, making sure it is even.
3. Roll the dowel carefully in the paper until you can no longer see the glue.
4. Repeat for the right edge.
5. Let dry.

For a paper clasp:

6. Use a piece of lightweight paper 2" x approximately 8", grained long. Fold the paper in half lengthwise, wrong sides together (if there is a wrong side). Open.
7. Fold the edges in to the middle fold, making the paper thinner. Open.
8. Spread a thin layer of glue on the middle two sections of the paper. Refold the edges in to the middle fold and press down.
9. Spread a thin layer of glue on the paper again, on top of one of these folded edges.
10. Fold the paper in half, making it even longer and thinner. Press it flat with a bone folder.
11. Take this glued paper and center it at the back of the scroll. Bring each side up and around so that they almost cross each other. Leave a comfortable margin (about $1/4$" to $1/2$").
12. Make marks on the glued paper where the two parts of the paper will meet.
13. With scissors, make a vertical slit at each of the marks; one slit should go halfway down and one slit should go halfway up.
14. Wrap this paper clasp around the scrolls, carefully sliding the top slit into the bottom slit. Trim the ends if desired.

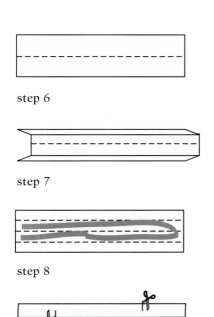

step 6

step 7

step 8

step 13

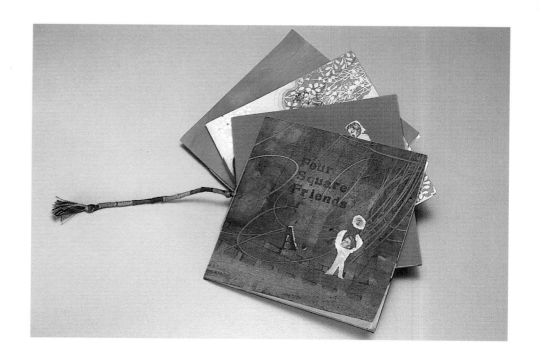

Four Square Friends, 2000; rubber-stamped text, collage, friendship strings; unique; 4^1/$_4$" x 4^1/$_2$"

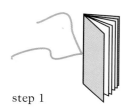

step 1

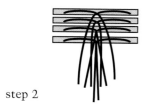

step 2

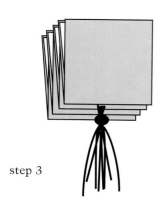

step 3

FOUR PAMPHLETS JOINED WITH A FRIENDSHIP STRING
(SEWING, WRAPPING)

My daughter came home from camp one summer caught up in the "friendship string" craze. I liked the possibility of using the string in a binding. *Four Square Friends* utilizes four pamphlets, each bound with a single signature, and with long embroidery-thread tails left intact. The friendship string is created by wrapping the tails from each of the pamphlets into one patterned tail.

Tools: heavy-duty needle with eye large enough for embroidery thread, four colors of embroidery thread, binder clip, scissors, cardboard (to protect the table when you poke holes in the pamphlets)
Materials: 8 sheets of text-weight 5^1/$_2$" x 8^1/$_2$", grained short, 4 sheets of heavier-weight paper 5^3/$_4$" x 8^3/$_4$" for the covers, grained short

  1. Before you begin, plan to leave a one-foot tail out of the middle hole. Starting from the outside, sew each of the pamphlets individually, using embroidery thread for the single-signature binding (see Materials and Methods: Sewing, Knots and Stitches, page 143). Use approximately three feet of thread. When you finish, again leave one foot of thread.
  2. Clip all the pamphlets together at the head. The pamphlets should all be facing the same way, with their spines aligned.
  3. Make one overhand knot (see page 142).

Note: as you wrap the outermost thread, you will need to hold tightly to the "core" threads.

4. Take one thread and wind it five times around all the other threads (as if they were one thread; this is the core).

5. Take another thread, pull it out of the bundle, and wrap it five times around all the threads, including the first thread (the core threads will change as you continue).

6. Proceed with each of the colors, one at a time, to create a pattern. When you come to a color you have already used, choose the longer of the two threads available.

7. To finish, wrap the last thread, then place it over the core and bring the end through to make a knot; see diagram.

8. Tie one last overhand knot.

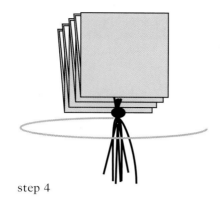

step 4

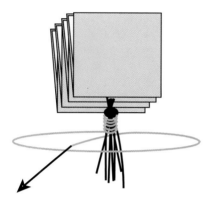

step 7

WINDOW BOOK
(GLUING)

After my toddler-aged son was seriously injured, I couldn't bring myself to go out into the world; it was too painful to see children running around when he was unable to move. When a nurse was available to care for my son, I sat in my studio and stared at my papers and knives, needles and scissors instead of taking a walk or trying to do something "fun." *It Is Safe in Here* is based on that time. I used the window book because it was a private and protected place to put my vulnerable feelings.

Materials: four pieces of 4-ply museum board 5" x 5^1/$_2$", grained long; one spine piece 5^1/$_2$" x ^{1}/$_4$", grained long; two cover papers 7^1/$_2$" x 12", grained short; two inner cover papers 5^1/$_4$" x 10^1/$_2$", grained short; two strips of inner paper 1^1/$_2$" x 5^1/$_4$", grained long

It Is Safe in Here, 2000; paper, collage, laser-printed text; unique; 5^1/$_2$" x 5"

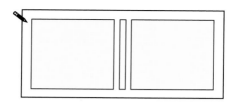

steps 1, 2 and 3

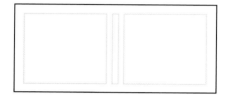

step 4

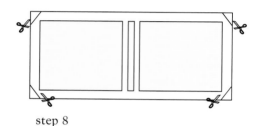

step 8

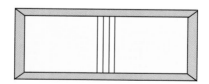

step 9

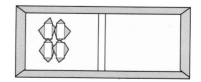

step 10

step 17 and 18

Tools: pencil, scissors, glue (or glue stick or paste), ruler, cutting mat, art knife, scrap paper, bone folder, waxed paper, heavy book

1. Put a piece of cover paper horizontally and wrong-side up on top of some scrap paper.

2. Arrange these pieces on top of the cover paper in a horizontal line from left to right: board, spine piece, board. Leave a one-inch margin from the left, top, and bottom edges of the cover paper. Leave $3/16$" between the spine piece and each of the boards.

3. With a pencil, draw lines around the boards and spine piece.

4. Remove the boards and spine piece.

5. Apply glue, glue stick, or paste to the paper inside the penciled outlines. If using PVA glue, only apply glue inside one outline at a time.

6. Press down the boards and spine piece.

7. Turn the project over. With a bone folder, smooth down the paper onto the boards. So that you don't make marks on your project, you can put waxed paper between the project and the bone folder.

8. Turn it back over. Cut off the corners with scissors, leaving approximately $1/8$" space between diagonals and the board.

9. Spread glue on each of the flaps and turn them in, one by one. After gluing one or two flaps, or if your scrap paper gets messy, get new scrap paper and continue gluing.

10. Smooth down all paper.

11. Place the project between two sheets of waxed paper and put it under a heavy book while you continue working.

12. Cut a window in one of the remaining boards. The window can be a square or rectangle or a number of squares.

13. Put the other piece of cover paper horizontally and wrong-side up on top of some scrap paper.

14. Arrange the two boards on the cover paper so that there is a one-inch margin all the way around the edges of the cover paper. The gap between the boards will be approximately $1/2$".

15. Repeat steps 3–10 (omitting a spine piece this time).

16. To reveal the window completely, turn the covered boards over so you can see the hole you cut.

17. With an art knife, cut diagonals in the cover paper from each of the corners of the hole to the center.

18. Apply more glue, if necessary, and wrap the flaps over the edges of the hole, creating the complete window.

19. Take one inner paper and place it wrong-side up in front of you.

20. Put the set of boards with the window on top of it. Try to center the paper if you can.

21. With a pencil, draw around the interior of the window.

22. Remove the set of boards. Cut out the window in the inner paper, cutting slightly inside the lines.

23. Apply glue to the wrong side of the newly cut paper, leaving about a one-inch margin right and left with no adhesive.

24. Align with the set of boards and rub down.

step 23

steps 28 and 29

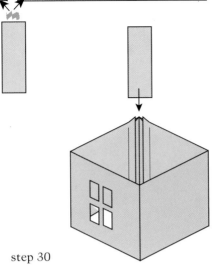

25. Repeat steps 23–24 with the first set of boards and spine piece.
26. Arrange the project in front of you wrong-side up: the set of boards with the spine piece is on your left, then the board with the window and its mate. The window should be the third panel from the left.
27. Put one spine strip wrong-side up on some scrap paper. Apply glue to it.
28. Lift up the unglued margin of the inner papers on each of the boards that you attached in step 23. Insert and smooth down the spine strip to connect the two sets.
29. Apply glue to each of the inner papers where it had no glue, and smooth it in place.
30. Repeat steps 27–29 to join the remaining sides into a box shape.
31. The boards should be aligned so that when you fold the set without the spine piece it will nest nicely in the outer boards with the spine piece.

Note: For extra reinforcement, use two pieces of self-adhesive linen tape before you glue down the inner strips at step 28.

step 30

THEMES

Themes continue to inspire the shape of Katherine Ng's books such as her *Spirit Vessel*, which is filled with text and woven in the shape of a gourd.

Katherine Ng: *Spirit Vessel*, 1996; letterpress, paper woven strips; 4" x 4" x 4 1/2" (photo by K. Ng)

"*Spirit Vessel*, created from a Brody Arts Fund Fellowship, is a study of gourds used in various cultures: Asian, South American, African, and American. Using metal type, I hand set a list of these uses, then letterpress printed the list on both sides of one sheet of paper. I cut the page into strips of text, then "wove" them into a vessel using a method inspired by the God's Eye. The title is inspired by the Chinese and Japanese uses of gourds. In the Chinese culture, gourds were used to hold evil spirits. In the Japanese culture, gourds were used as containers for spirits intoxicating in nature. I was intrigued by the similar uses of gourds in the different cultures and decided to make that the focus of *Spirit Vessel*."

KATHERINE NG

CHAPTER 2

ACCORDION-FOLD BOOKS

Accordion-fold books are great to display since you can see the entire text at once, even if it is inside a glass case. The only drawback is that the book needs to be fairly short. A long accordion, when opened, is unwieldy and may fall over.

Because of all the variations, an accordion-fold book can provide great flexibility in sequence and pacing. You can add suspense to text or images with a change in paper color, change of sequence, or the addition of fold-out pages, signatures, cut-outs, or pop-ups. For example, add a miniature book in the middle of an exciting part. Or, if you have two related texts that can be read in either order, a back-to-back accordion would be a good structure to choose. Adapt any structure to fit your book's concept.

For some of these accordion-fold books you will need to know the single-signature binding. You will find it in Materials and Methods: Sewing, Knots and Stitches (page 143).

MINIATURE TABBED ACCORDION
(FOLDING, CUTTING)

I adapted this structure from a book written in Italian by Laura Badalucco called *Kirigami* (which is Japanese for a type of paper cutting). I don't know Italian. Or Japanese. From looking at the pictures I realized it was a type of pop-up structure. Then I modified it. In *Kirigami*, the book is made into an address book.

Tabbed Accordion model, 2001; acrylic inks, rubber stamps, gesso, graphite; 3" x 3"

Tools: ruler, pencil, art knife, cutting mat
Materials: text/lightweight paper 3" x 17", grained short, to make a book 2³/₄"
x 3" with three fore-edge tabs

1. Fold an eight-paneled accordion. (See page 140.)
2. Put the accordion in front of you horizontally so that the first fold is a valley fold.
3. Measure and score a vertical line ¹/₄" on either side of the folded edge of the first peak.
4. Repeat step 3 for the remaining two peak folds.
5. Measure and mark 1" down from the top of the first peak fold.
6. Cut a horizontal slit from the left score to the right score at the first peak fold.
7. Measure 1" down from the top and 2" down from the top of the second peak fold.
8. Cut horizontal slits at these two places on the second peak fold.
9. Measure 2" down at the third peak fold, and make a horizontal slit.
10. Refold the fore edges so that the little tab sticks out and has a peak fold in the center (it pops out); the rest of the fore edge bends inward.
11. Attach a wrapped hard cover or separate boards (see Materials and Methods: Covers and Dust Jackets, pages 140 and 148).

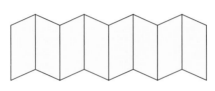

step 1

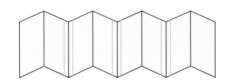

steps 3, 4

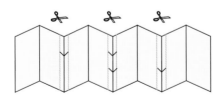

steps 6, 7, 8, and 9

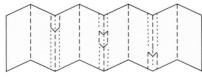

step 10

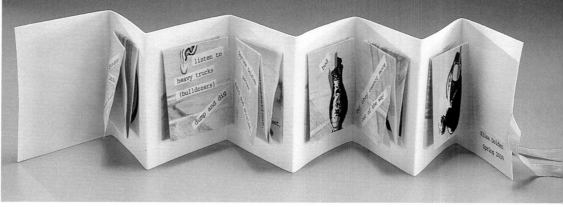

Daytime Daisies, 2000; paste paper, collage, laser-printed text; unique; 2³/4" x 3"

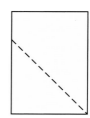

step 1

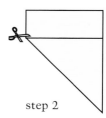

step 2

step 4

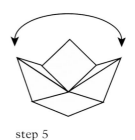

step 5

ACCORDION BOOK WITH FLOWER-FOLD PAGES
(FOLDING, GLUING)

My daughter made a book like this in elementary school. I like the way the pages expand. I used this structure for *Daytime Daisies,* which is about daisies growing and dying while children play in the dirt at their feet and bulldozers move dirt at the construction site nearby. It is a metaphor for the way we are sometimes rooted in one place watching everything, unable to move except through our children. The following example has four panels.

Tools: metal-edged ruler and art knife, cutting mat, bone folder
Materials: 1 sheet of paper cut to 4¹/2" x 18" (cardstock or heavier weight like Canson Mi Teintes), 4 sheets of 8¹/2" x 11" medium weight paper (not cardstock)

To make a square from rectangular paper:
 1. Fold each piece of the four 8¹/2" x 11" medium-weight papers on the diagonal so that the edges align (see diagram).
 2. Cut across the edge that is not doubled. You should now have a triangle left over.
 3. Open the triangle. It is now a perfect 8¹/2" square. Turn it over so that the peak is facing up.

Continue to make the flower-fold pages:
 4. Fold the square in half one way. Open. Fold in half the other way. You will have two valley folds on this side and one peak fold.
 5. Bring up the corners of each end of the diagonal fold. Match them.
 6. Press down one flat square to meet the opposite flat square. You now have a folded 4¹/4" square.

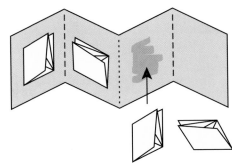

7. Fold all four squares. Set aside.
8. Fold the longer paper in half widthwise.
9. Fold each end back and match it to the fold. You should have three alternating peak and valley folds.
10. Arrange the long folded cover strip so that it begins with a valley fold.
11. Since the folded square pages will open out from the corner, decide if you want the page to open up or down. To open up, place the open corner in the bottom left or right corner. To open down, position the open corner in the top left or right corner. Put glue on one of the flat sides of one of the 4¹/4" squares. Press into place, centered on the first section of the cover strip.
12. Repeat with other three squares in second, third, and fourth sections.

Note: In the diagram, pages one and three open *up* and pages two and four open *down*.

steps 10, 11, and 12

TRIANGLE BOOK WITH SQUARE HARD COVERS
(FOLDING, SLITTING, GLUING)

I used this structure for *The Golden Beak,* a dark story of a cat who wishes to catch a bird with a golden beak for the status of owning the golden beak. The triangular pages give the image of the beak. The covers are purple velvet with a bit of shiny gold paper that evokes the feeling of luxury. I pasted the gold paper over a small window before the cover was complete. To help me position the windows in each of the forty-four covers of the edition I used a template.

The Golden Beak, 1998; letterpress printed text, velvet, paper; edition of 44; 3" x 3"

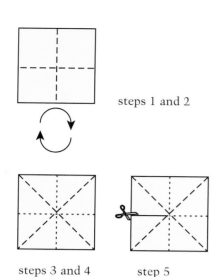

steps 1 and 2

steps 3 and 4   step 5

Tools: pencil, ruler, scissors, art knife, cutting mat, glue/paste, waxed paper, bone folder, old magazines for scrap paper, heavy book for a weight

Materials: text paper is a square piece of medium-weight paper (example: 5" x 5"); for the covers you will need five squares of 4-ply museum board $2^3/4$" x $2^3/4$", a piece of $1/8$" wide ribbon approximately two inches long, four pieces of book cloth or paper-backed cloth $3^1/4$", one square of $3^1/4$" x $3^1/4$" inner paper.

For the text paper:

1. Fold the square in half. Open.
2. Fold the square in half the other way. Open. Turn the paper over.
3. Fold the paper diagonally. Open.
4. Fold the paper diagonally the other way. Open.
5. From one straight (non-diagonal) fold, cut a slit to the very center.
6. Accordion-fold (alternating peaks and valleys) the paper into a triangle.

For the square covers:

7. Orient all the boards and papers and book cloth so the grain is going the same way.
8. Cut one of the square boards diagonally, to make two triangles. The other four boards should remain square.
9. With one square of the book cloth wrong-side up, apply glue or paste. And immediately place a piece of board in the center. Press down.
10. Cut diagonals across the corners.
11. Fold up the edges and wrap around the board, one side at a time, in any order. Try to remember which way the grain is going.
12. Place between two sheets of waxed paper and put under weights while you cover the three other square boards, one at a time. Put each in waxed paper and under weights as you go. Draw an arrow on the waxed paper in the direction of the grain.

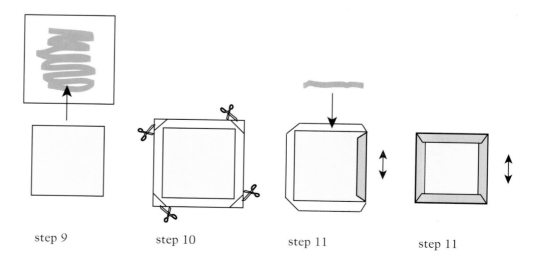

step 9   step 10   step 11   step 11

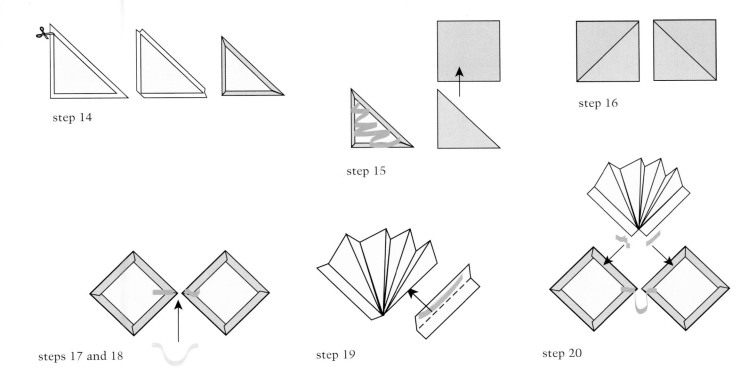

step 14

step 15

step 16

steps 17 and 18

step 19

step 20

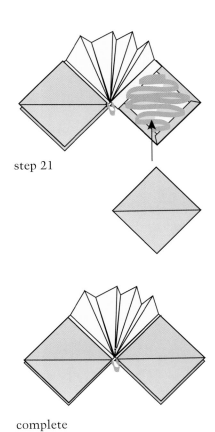

step 21

complete

13. Cut the inner cover paper in half diagonally, making two triangles.

14. Apply glue and press down one of the triangular pieces of board. Cut the corners. Wrap the triangles. Repeat for the second set of triangles.

15. Take out one of the wrapped squares. To the back of one of the triangles, apply glue, then affix to the *front* of the wrapped square.

16. Repeat for the other triangle. Put these back under the weights.

17. Take out the remaining two wrapped squares and place them wrong-side up in front of you as if they were two diamonds with one of each of their points $1/4$" from the other.

18. Apply glue to the squares in a short, horizontal line across the points. Press the piece of ribbon down here. The ribbon will not be attached to the boards at the $1/4$" gap.

19. Fold the $2^1/2$" x 1" paper strips in half lengthwise. Apply glue in a thin, flat line to half of one strip. Press the strip to one of the cut edges of the inner folded paper. Repeat for the other strip.

20. Apply glue to the backs of the tabs on the inner folded paper. Position the tabs so that their folded edges will hang off the boards $1/16$"–$1/8$" (the width of the covered boards). This will allow the book to close properly.

21. Apply glue to the back of one of the remaining boards and press down so that the raised triangle is at the bottom of the diamond shape. Repeat for the last board. The folded pages should rest in the lowered section when the book is closed.

22. Place waxed paper between the last folded pages at each end of the book and the covered boards. Close the book and press it under weights.

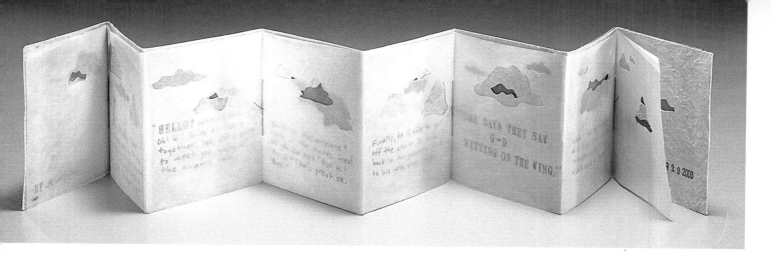

On the Wing, 2000; paper, rubber-stamped text; unique; $2^{3}/4$" x 3"

LAYERED ACCORDION BOOK
(FOLDING, CUTTING, SEWING)

In a newspaper article about immigrants, one man called his French passport the "green snake." The passport was made of green paper in an accordion format and rubber-stamped: a "found" artist's book.

For the layered accordion book, you will need three sheets of lightweight paper each 24" long. You can also make a tiny book for practice out of an $8^{1}/2$" x 11" sheet cut into thirds lengthwise. I recommend a colored or painted paper for the bottom layer and two sheets of translucent paper such as drafting film for the top two layers. You may also choose three sheets of colored paper into which you have cut shaped holes so the previous colors show through.

Tools: awl, corrugated cardboard, needle, thread, ruler, pencil, binder clip
Materials: three pieces of paper (see above) 5" x 24", grained short, two foreedge strips 5" x 2", grained long
Example: 3" x 5" book

1. Fold paper into an accordion with eight segments (see Materials and Methods: Folds, p. 140).
2. Make all cuts, rubber stamps, illustrations, or other marks on the papers now. Let dry, if necessary.
3. With the valley fold as the first fold from the left, nest all the pages from bottom to top. Secure all three sheets with a binder clip placed at the edge of one of the panels. Make sure the binder clip has a small pad of protective scrap paper under it so it does not directly touch and dent your book.
4. Measure and poke three holes in the first valley fold. Put one hole equidistant from the head and tail of the book, the other holes each one inch from the center hole. Sew a single signature. (See Materials and Methods: Knots and Stitches, page 143.)
5. Poke holes in the next valley fold and repeat step 8, using the same mea-

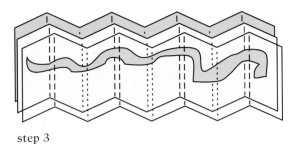

step 3

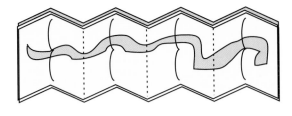

steps 4 and 5

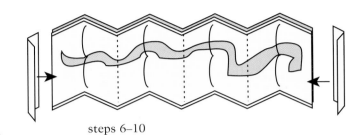

steps 6–10

surements for hole placement so the stitching will match from one signature to the next. Repeat for the third and fourth valley folds.

For a more finished look:
6. Take two strips of the colored paper the same height as your book (5" in this example) and 2" wide.
7. Fold each paper in half lengthwise to make it long and narrow.
8. Put a line of glue or glue stick on the side with the valley fold.
9. Close your book by folding it up completely. Now take one of the strips and face the open edge to the left and the folded edge to the right. Adhere the strip around the three layers of the first section only. The book is now contained at the fore edge (see diagram for steps 6–10).
10. Repeat for the last section (the back of the book) and the last strip.

Variation: Use one layer that is approximately 1" shorter and a second layer that is approximately 2" shorter for a more three-dimensional look resembling Julie Chen's *Radio Silence*.

Julie Chen: *Radio Silence*, 1995; letterpress printed on a variety of papers including found objects; boxed edition of 75 copies (box not shown); 5" x 3¹/₂" x 2¹/₄" when closed and expandable to a full length of 7 feet

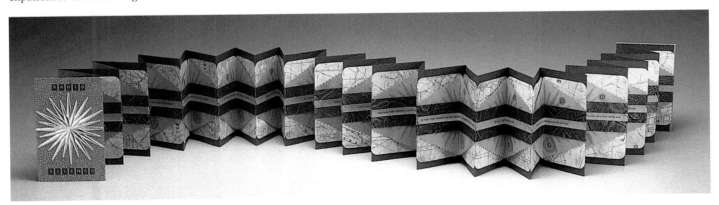

Val Simonetti: *B-babble,* 1984; letterpress printed text, silkscreen; edition of 17; closed: 6³/₄" x 8", open: 6³/₄" x 34"

BACK-TO-BACK ACCORDION BOOK
(FOLDING, SEWING)

My friend Val used this structure many years ago to make a book for her new niece, Bianca, called *B-babble.* The book had many words beginning with the letter B.

 "What I like about this particular structure is that it comes close to being a continuous loop. It has a title page, but I notice that people are often unsure just where the text begins. Since I made *B-babble* to celebrate the arrival of the only child of my only sister, it seems appropriate that there is no logical conclusion to it. The gestation period for this piece was roughly parallel to that of my niece. I made the silkscreen pages about a year in advance, more as a formal exercise than anything else.

"About the same time I took a weeklong workshop with Karen Zukor as part of the California College of Arts & Crafts Extension series. Karen showed us some really intriguing book structures, which were the inspiration for several subsequent book designs, including this one.

"I had also been longing to take advantage of CCAC's diverse collection of type; something with short chunks of text seemed in order. I could have easily spent the next few decades looking for just the right phrase to set in Futura & Co., but luckily Bianca was born before that project had progressed very far.

"After she and I were introduced, the book appeared in a rush; surely the fastest I've ever worked in the absence of a deadline. Both Bianca and *B-babble* turned sixteen this summer. I can't say whether she was more pleased than baffled to have an auntish hymn of adoration cum type specimen book created in her honor; so far she just seems to have taken it in stride."

VAL SIMONETTI

For this particular version you will only see six pages on each side. Keep the ends blank. For more pages, follow the instructions for the back-to-back accordion with tunnel (page 35), but do not cut out any holes.

Tools: pencil, bone folder, needle, thread, binder clip, a folded piece of scrap paper

Materials: Two pieces of 24" x 5^1/$_2$" paper, grained short. Choose one type of cover. **For a hard cover:** two pieces of 4-ply board 5^3/$_4$" x 6^1/$_4$", grained short, two pieces of 8^1/$_4$" x 7^3/$_4$" bookcloth or cover paper, grained short
For a flexible, non-adhesive cover: two 3" x 5^1/$_2$" of 2-ply boards, two pieces of 5" x 5^1/$_2$" paper, grained long, two pieces of 7^1/$_2$" x 3" paper, grained short, one spine piece of medium-weight paper 3" x 5^1/$_2$", grained long
Example: 6^1/$_4$" x 5^3/$_4$" book

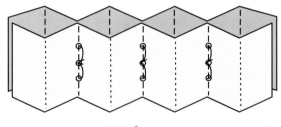

step 2

1. Make two accordions from the 24" x 5^1/$_2$" paper with eight small segments each. (See Materials and Methods: Folds, page 140.)
2. Place accordions in front of you with their backs together so that the first folds are peak folds.
3. Keeping them together, flatten the accordions and clip them together.
4. Measure, mark, and poke three holes at each of the valley folds: one centered, one measured 1^1/$_2$" up from the center hole, and then one measured 1^1/$_2$" down from the center hole. These holes should be in the second, fourth, and sixth folds.

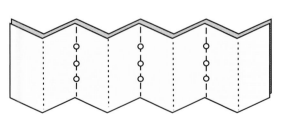

steps 3 and 4

step 6

5. Sew the accordions together as if you were sewing a single signature in each of these three valley folds.
6. After sewing, reverse the folds of the back accordion so that peaks of both accordions meet at the sewing.

For hard covers:
7. Cover two separate boards with cloth or paper. See Materials and Methods: Glued Hard Covers, page 148, for additional help.
8. Cut diagonals at the corners.
9. Fold down the edges, one by one.
10. Repeat steps 8 and 9 for the second board.
11. Place the folded papers in front of you so that they are accordion-folded and closed. The top layer should have an open middle and folded right and left edges.

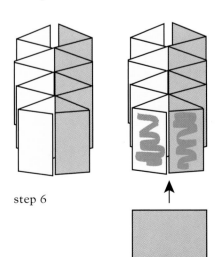

step 6

steps 11 and 12

The Road Unfolded, 2000; rubber-stamped text, acrylic paint, torn maps; unique; 5" x 5"

12. Apply glue to the top pages. Align the front cover and press it down.
13. Turn the book over. Repeat steps 11 and 12 for the back cover, trying to align it with the front cover as well.
14. Place waxed paper between the covers and the front and back sheets. Press under a heavy weight overnight.

For non-adhesive, flexible covers:

 1. See instructions in Materials and Methods: Wrapped Hard Cover, page 140. For the front and back of this book, the open edges will be on the long sides.

 2. Place the spine piece in front of you vertically. Mark the spine piece in the center 1 1/2" from either edge.

 3. Measure and mark 1/8" on either side of the center mark. Score two lines that are parallel to the long side of the spine piece.

 4. Insert the spine piece into the wrapped covers, connecting them.

 5. If it seems too tight, cut slight diagonals at each of the corners. See diagram.

 6. Insert the accordion-folded book into the wrapped covers at the right and left edges.

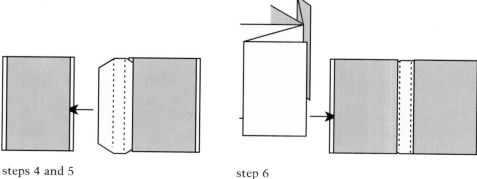

steps 4 and 5   step 6

BACK-TO-BACK ACCORDION BOOK WITH TUNNEL

(FOLDING, CUTTING, SEWING)

I adapted the previous structure to make a tunnel book for *No Moon Tonight*. The gray side has a story of insomnia. The translucent side has the names of each season's full moons.

The structure works best when all accordions are made from the same weight of paper. Use medium- or heavy-weight paper for best results. I used a lighter weight, translucent paper for one side of the accordion, which looks nice but doesn't sit up quite as well when the book is opened. I decided that the translucent paper was important to my concept of "moonness," so I used it anyway. If you do use translucent paper you will need to add endpapers (see step 17). You can make this book longer by adding more inner papers and paper strips to connect them.

Tools: pencil, bone folder, needle, thread, binder clip, a folded piece of scrap paper

Materials: four pieces of 12" x 5$\frac{1}{2}$" paper, grained short, two paper strips 5$\frac{1}{2}$" x 1", grained long. **For the cover:** two pieces of 4-ply board 5$\frac{3}{4}$" x 6$\frac{1}{4}$", grained short, two pieces of 8$\frac{1}{4}$" x 7$\frac{3}{4}$" bookcloth or cover paper, grained short.

Example: 6$\frac{1}{4}$" x 5$\frac{3}{4}$" book

1. Fold the four pieces of paper into accordions of four panels each.
2. Fold the paper strips in half lengthwise.
3. Apply glue to the back of one of the paper strips.

No Moon Tonight, 1999; letterpress printed text, book cloth, paper; edition of 35; 6$\frac{1}{4}$" x 5$\frac{1}{4}$" (photo by Jim Hair)

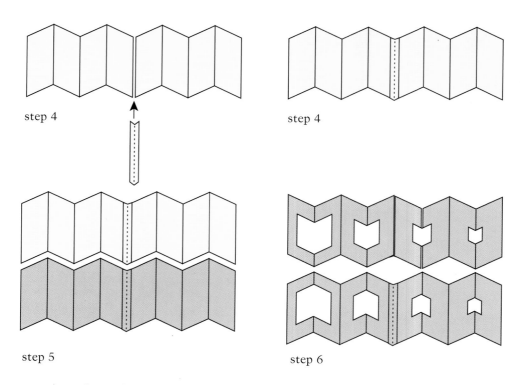

step 4

step 4

step 5

step 6

4. Press the end of one of the accordions on one half of the strip. Press the end of another accordion to the other half of the strip.

5. Repeat steps 3 and 4 for the other two accordions and the other paper strip. Do not connect these two accordions to the first two accordions.

6. For a tunnel effect on one side only, take one of the sets of accordions and cut shapes in the valley folds from large to small. (Repeat the same shapes for the other set of accordions if you want the tunnel to be symmetrical.)

To sew:

7. Place the accordions in front of you horizontally and with their backs together.

8. Flatten them and clip them together.

9. Measure, mark, and poke four holes at each of the valley folds so that you have a pair of holes above the hole for your tunnel and a pair below. These should be on each of four valley folds. See diagram.

10. Sew the accordions together with one stitch at the top and one stitch at the bottom. Tie off each with a square knot.

11. After sewing, take the back accordion and reverse the folds so that the peaks of both accordions meet at the sewing.

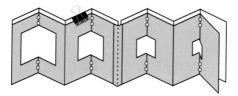

steps 7, 8, and 9

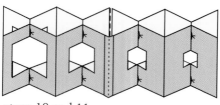

steps 10 and 11

step 13

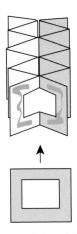

For the hard covers:

12. Using your art knife against a metal ruler, cut a window in the top cover board.

13. Glue and cover the boards. For the window board you will need to cut an "x" from corner to corner of the window. Cut a rectangle 1/2" inside the window. Fold the cloth or paper over the edges of the window.

14. Place the inner folded papers in front of you so that they are closed (the top piece should have a folded middle and open right and left edges).

15. Apply glue to the top pages. Press the front cover board down, aligned.

16. Turn the book over. Repeat steps 14 and 15 for the back cover, trying to align it with the front cover as well.

steps 14 and 15

If you are using translucent paper:

17. Cut out a window in the endsheet that matches half the window in your front board. Apply glue and press over the translucent paper that is already adhered to the board. See the details in the photo of *No Moon Tonight*.

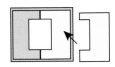

step 17

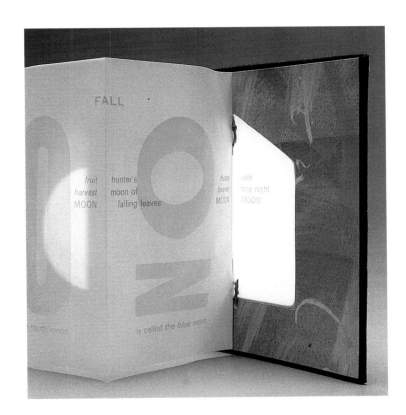

No Moon Tonight, detail

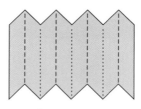

step 1

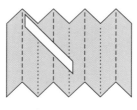

step 2

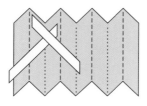

step 3

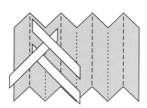

step 4

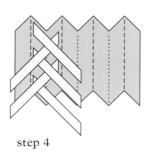

step 4

Fortune Book, 1997; paper, fortunes; unique; 3" x 3"

FLAG BOOK WITH FORTUNES
(FOLDING, GLUING)

Tools: glue stick or PVA, magazines for scrap paper
Materials: 3^1/$_2$" x 8" piece of medium-weight paper, 15 fortunes from cookies (or ^{1}/$_4$"–^{1}/$_2$" x 2^1/$_4$" paper strips)

  1. Fold the paper into an accordion with eight segments (see Materials and Methods: Folds, page 140).
  2. Apply glue stick or a dot of PVA to the back of the first fortune (the glue will be on the far right on the back). Press the first fortune down just a tiny bit below the top edge of the accordion on the front of the first fold.
  3. Apply glue stick or a dot of PVA to the back of the second fortune (this time on the far left on the back). Press the second fortune down on the *back* of the first fold just below the first fortune.
  4. Repeat steps 2 and 3 for the third, fourth, and fifth fortunes on the first fold.
  5. Repeat steps 2 and 3 for all the fortunes on the second and third folds.
  6. Using 3" x 2^1/$_2$" boards, grained long, attach a wrapped hard cover (see Materials and Methods: Folds, page 140) or separate boards and endpapers (Materials and Methods: Glued Hard Covers, page 148). If you make the latter, adhere the ends of the accordion to the boards before adhering the inner paper in step 7.

THREE-PANEL JACOB'S LADDER BOOK
(GLUING)

I first saw a two-panel book like this made by Coriander Reisbord. A three-paneled version behaves like an accordion because of the alternating peaks and valleys. However, the three-panel Jacob's ladder is different because it is made up of many layers, rather than a single sheet of folded paper.

My first mock-ups for this book were made of cereal-box cardboard and laser-printer paper.

Tools: ruler, pencil, glue, glue brush, scrap paper, waxed paper
Materials: six $2^1/2$" x 5" boards, grained long, six 11" x $1^1/2$" strips of paper, grained short, or three 11" ribbons. If you use ribbons, skip step 1.
Example: $2^1/2$" x 5"

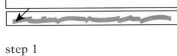

step 1

1. Prepare the strips by applying glue to the back of one strip of paper and adhering it to the back of another one. Repeat for two more strips. You may do this step in advance. Place the strips under a heavy weight overnight.
2. Line up your boards in pairs. *Top row:* front cover, board, board; *bottom row:* board, board, back cover.

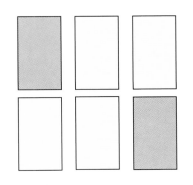

step 2

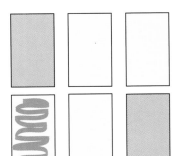

step 3

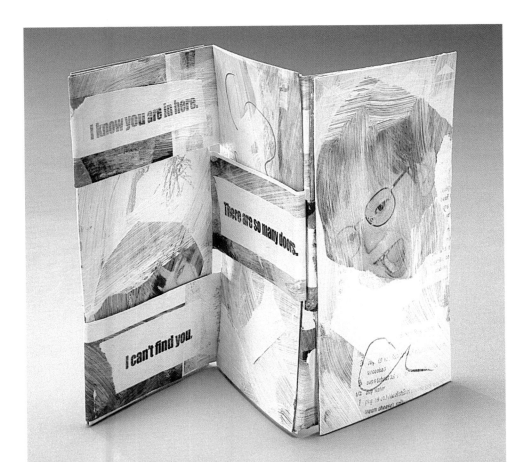

I Know You Are in Here, 2000; photocopies, acrylics; Jacob's ladder; unique; $2^3/4$" x 5"

39

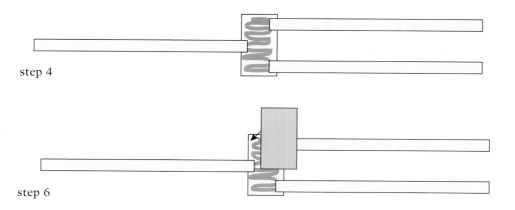

step 4

step 6

3. Brush a thin layer of glue on the wrong side of the left board in the bottom row (as arranged in step 2).

4. Apply glue to the end of one paper strip (about one inch). Repeat for the other two strips. Glue the three paper strips to the board as follows: one strip facing left, centered, and the other two strips facing right, positioned top and bottom (about $1/8$" from the head and tail).

5. Take the left board of the top row, and apply glue completely to the back of it.

6. Glue it down to the first board, sandwiching the strips.

7. Flip the glued boards over so that the front cover is facedown. (The middle strip now faces right and the two strips face left.)

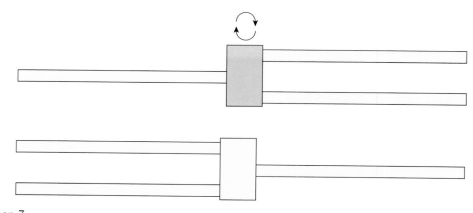

step 7

8. Fold the top and bottom strips to the right, over the board.

9. Glue the top and bottom strips to the middle board of the bottom row (of step 2). Leave a $1/4$" margin between the boards from the first set and the boards from the second set.

Julie Chen: *Space-Time Geometry,* 1996, illustrations by David Turner; edition of 10 copies; letterpress printing and color photocopy; closed: 5" x 11" x 6¹/₂" (depth), open: 30"

10. Pull the middle strip out from underneath. Fold it to the left.
11. Place the other board of the second set wrong-side up (if there is an unpainted or wrong side) on top of all three paper strips on the left.

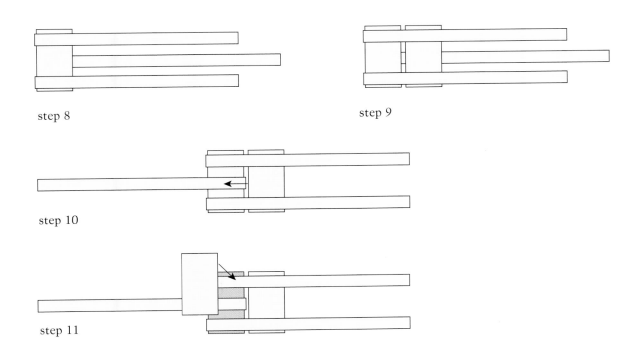

step 8

step 9

step 10

step 11

12. Wrap the middle strip (by folding over to the right) and glue it down to the left board only. This is the back of the second board.

13. Tuck the middle strip completely under the board to the back.

14. Glue the second set of halves together by flipping the left board over to the right; the glued-down strips are hidden inside the sandwich.

15. Place the bottom of the third set of boards (from the top row) under the middle strip. Glue the middle strip down across the board to the right. Leave a $1/4$" margin between the boards from the second set and boards from the third set.

16. Wrap the top and bottom strips back to the left. Glue down to the right board.

17. Glue the top of the third set (this is the back cover) on top of all three strips.

18. Making sure both covers (no strips across them) are on the outside, accordion-fold the book. Align the boards as you make one a peak fold and the other a valley fold.

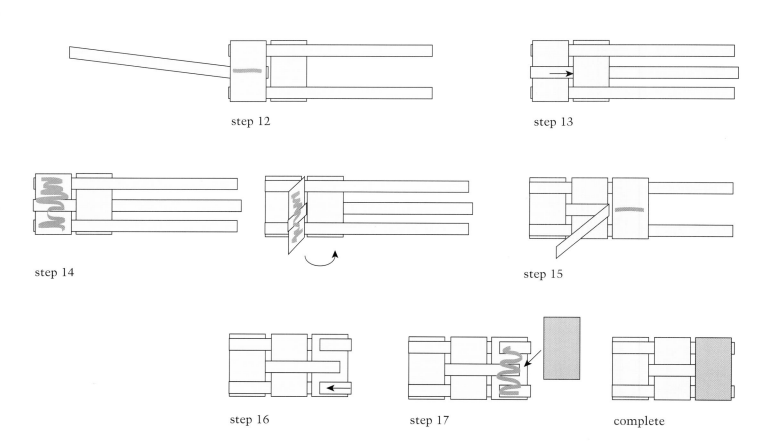

step 12

step 13

step 14

step 15

step 16

step 17

complete

CHAPTER 3

POCKET BOOKS

Books with pockets contain mysteries: you don't know what is hidden inside. By not revealing everything at once, you can work with multiple ideas. Betsy Davids found that paper bags made a perfect medium for telling a many-layered story.

Betsy Davids: *Once and Future Travels*, 1992; maps, photographs, mixed media, computer-generated text; 9" x 12"

Betsy Davids: *Five-Year Journals: December 1997: Heart Needlework;* photographs, postcards, receipts, handwritten text, mixed media; 5¹/₂" x 7"; *May-June 1997;* paper ephemera, handwritten text; 6" x 8¹/₂"

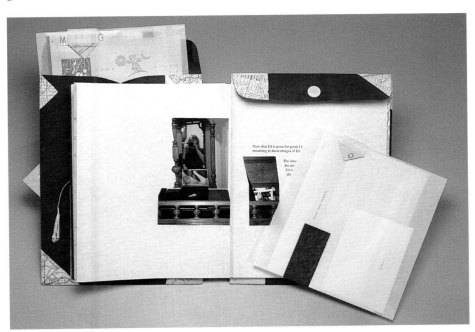

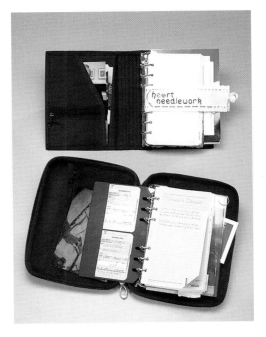

Betsy Davids: *Sites and Passages,* 1990-1992; water bottle tops, journal writing, photos, printed paper ephemera; notebook; 7" x 9¹/₂"

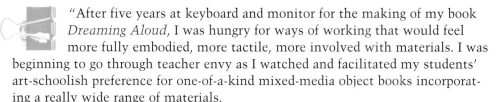

"After five years at keyboard and monitor for the making of my book *Dreaming Aloud,* I was hungry for ways of working that would feel more fully embodied, more tactile, more involved with materials. I was beginning to go through teacher envy as I watched and facilitated my students' art-schoolish preference for one-of-a-kind mixed-media object books incorporating a really wide range of materials.

"Then, for nine months I was away from home and studio. I had to work with the limited resources of the traveler: materials that were portable or found, small tools, my hands as primary tool. No type. No presses. I was especially attracted to the printed paper ephemera of travel, the ordinary stuff that is so everyday but so exotic in another language and culture. Every time I travel, I desire to keep that stuff, and the usual result is domestic clutter. This time I made a bargain with myself: I could hang on to every single ticket, map, bag that came into my hands, if I made books with them.

"The first results were begun in Greece and finished at home. *Sites & Passages* is a book of journal writing, snapshots, and printed paper stuff in a found notebook. *Excess Baggage* is a big, sloppy, excessive, textless book composed entirely of paper bags, plastic bags, receipts, daily spending records, maps, and travel-worn socks and pants, all sewn into a concertina spine.

"These travel books gave rise to a series of bag books, most of them using a simpler structure I devised of same-size bag folios joined at the fore edge with a slightly larger bag wrapped around as cover. I like that bag structure because it's so self-evident (great for teaching beginners). The bag openings create pockets, compartments, in which things can be put that can be pulled out and read or handled, and the bags also create page surfaces. Personal contents can be

Betsy Davids: *Turning Into a Pumpkin,* 1994; assemblage with photos, postcards and paper bags; unique; 8¹/₄" x 7¹/₄"

secluded in the pockets and flaps, and more general public content can go on the bag surface pages. The outside bag surfaces carry the more accessible contents, so that even a superficial viewing will yield something, but a longer, deeper viewing will yield much more. I also like embedding the actual artifacts from lived experience into the book about them.

"In *Turning Into a Pumpkin* the viewer who doesn't want to know about my spiritual longings and my dream life doesn't have to unfold and decipher the handwritten journal texts inside the bag pockets. But the layers are there. When I recently typed out that book's entire text for a show, the conversion from handwriting inside bag pockets to typography on linear pages put the content much more in the reader's face and flattened the reading experience. The specific source material is a series of pilgrimages to ancient dream-healing and snake-cult sites in Greece and Crete, related dreams, and pumpkins carved from the dream images. Inside the bags are a narrative about the journey written on postcards and several journal passages expressing my feelings and insights.

"Part of what sustains my interest with the bag structure is the implicit myth of transformation, redemption, reclamation. The lowly bag becomes an Artist Book, thereby creating a context for acts of remembering and celebrating."

BETSY DAVIDS

PAPER BAG BOOK
(SEWING)

Tools: bookbinding needle, thread
Materials: three lunch-size paper bags, postcards, other ephemera

1. Fold each bag in half widthwise.
2. Nest them one inside the other, alternating the open sides with the bottom flaps. One bag may be facing left (open) and another may be facing right.
3. Poke five holes in the spine through all the bags and sew a single signature (See page 143), or machine-sew a line down the centerfold.
4. Write on the bags and add things to the pockets.

Note: A very thick book may not stay closed. To secure it you may want to tie a piece of ribbon around it. Betsy Davids used a flexible tape measure and a little truck with a magnet to contain *GerTRUDES & TRUCKS*. Her book incorporates a three-way dream exchange by mail about Gertrude Stein, grandmothers, trucks, and femininity.

Variation: To make a book like Betsy's, use PVA, glue stick, or staples, and attach the back of one folded bag to the front of the next one. Use a larger bag for a wraparound cover if desired.

Left: Betsy Davids: *GerTRUDES & TRUCKS*, 1994; bakery bags, rubber stamps, handwriting, photocopies, tape measure, refrigerator magnet; mini-edition of two; 7" x 6$\frac{1}{2}$" x 2"
Right: Betsy Davids: *The New Studio Dream: A Visit from Mrs. G.*, 1995; rubber stamps, handwriting, colored pencil on paper bag with button and rubber-band closure; mini edition of two in basket (basket not shown); 4 $^{3}/_{4}$" x 7"

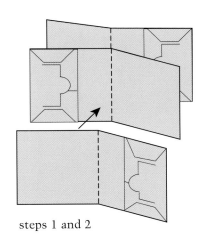

steps 1 and 2

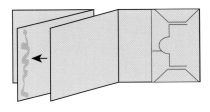

variation

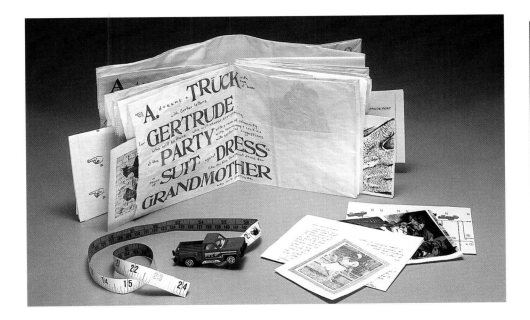

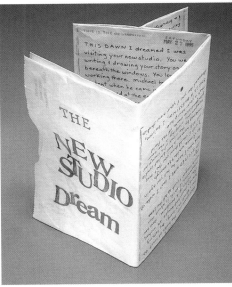

SINGLE-PAGE BOOK WITH POCKETS

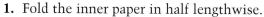

(FOLDING, SLITTING, GLUING)

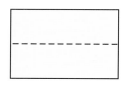

step 1

Tools: ruler, bone folder (optional), pencil, scissors or art knife, glue or glue stick
Materials: Inner paper: $8^1/2"$ x 11" lightweight paper; **Outer wrapper:** $2^3/4"$ x 6", grained short
Example: $2^1/2"$ x $2^3/4"$ book

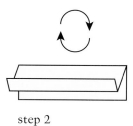

step 2

1. Fold the inner paper in half lengthwise.
2. With the folded edge at the top, fold a single layer from the bottom edge up $1^1/2"$.
3. Turn the paper over and fold the matching bottom single edge up $1^1/2"$.
4. Open the paper but keep the pockets folded. With the pockets facedown on the table, fold $3/8"$ in from one of the open sides, making a tab.
5. Keeping the tab folded, fold the paper in half widthwise.
6. Accordion-fold both edges back to the middle fold.
7. Open the paper up. Cut along the lengthwise fold from the first vertical fold to the third vertical fold (See diagram).

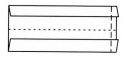

step 3

step 4

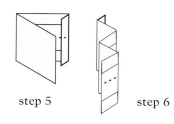

step 5   step 6

Admit One, 2000; tickets, paper, rubberstamped text; unique; $2^1/4"$ x $2^1/2"$

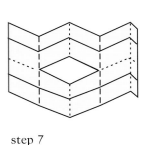

step 7

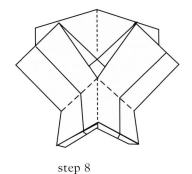

step 8

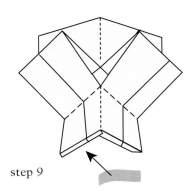

step 9

8. Pinch the two middle squares on the right and the two middle squares on the left. See the diagram. The tabs should be inside.

9. Put glue along one of the tabs, and adhere the tabs to each other.

10. Push the ends in to the middle so that the project looks like an "X."

11. Flatten the "x". Fold it in half so that the glued, tabbed edge is inside.

For the outer wrapper:

12. Measure and fold a $^3/8$" flap from each of the short ends. Hook these flaps around the text paper and crease a rounded fold in the middle. Glue down the flaps to the inner paper.

In my book *Admit One*, the tickets are loose, to permit the reader to rearrange them. If you use tickets or other papers and want to have a fixed order, you can number the loose papers and their corresponding book pages. Or, you can punch holes in the papers and punch holes at the top of each book page. Tie threads from the papers to the pages to hold them in place.

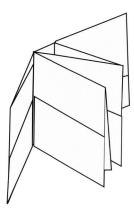

step 11

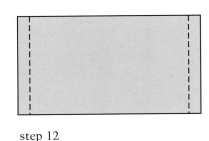

step 12

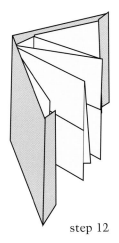

step 12

POCKET TRIANGLE
AND DIAMOND BOOK
(CUTTING)

My husband devised this method for joining the pages. It uses no adhesives or sewing. I based the pocket pages on a very elegant origami wallet found in *The Art of Origami* by Gay Merrill Gross. Although the simplified wallet page is less elegant than the original, it is easier to fold.

I used a double-sided paper for *Green Tea*; it is dark green on one side and a natural, bark-flecked color on the other. I did not have a text or a title when I began folding the pages. When the book was assembled I heard the title in my head. I folded glassine paper into tea bags and put them in the pockets, then attached the tea bag strings to the book so they would not fall out. Each tea bag contains a line of text and a small amount of real green tea. I made one mistake: although I like the look of the vertical title strip, the title should have been right-side up to cue the reader that this book is vertically oriented.

Tools: pencil, ruler, scissors or art knife and cutting mat, bone folder (optional), glue stick or glue

Materials: four sheets (or more) of lightweight paper, two pieces of 2-ply or 4-ply museum board slightly smaller than the finished book size, eight strips of paper the same height as the boards and the same color as the pockets by 2" wide.

Left: *Triangle Diamond Sample,* 2000; double-sided origami paper; unique; 1⁵/8" x 2¹/4"

Right: *Green Tea,* 2000; double-sided paper, glassine, laser-printed text, linen thread; unique; 4¹/4" x 5¹/4" x 2³/4" depth

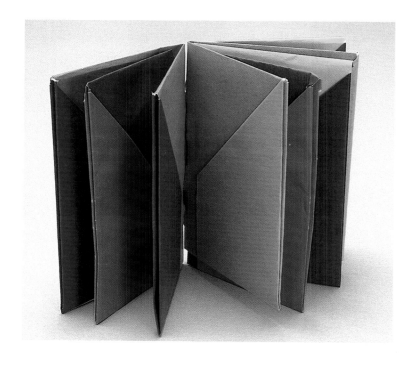

Green Tea, detail

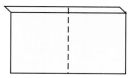

steps 1–4

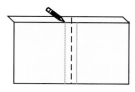

step 5

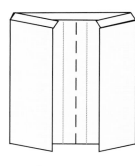

step 6

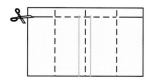

step 7

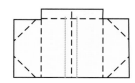

step 8

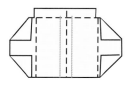

step 8

Here are some sample sizes:
Paper size: $5^3/4$" square origami paper **Book size:** $1^5/8$" x $2^1/4$"
Paper size: $8^1/2$" x 11" **Book size:** $2^7/8$" x $3^1/2$"
Paper size: $8^1/2$" x 14" **Book size:** $3^5/8$" square book
Paper size: 11" x 17" **Book size:** approximately $4^1/4$" x $5^1/4$". The following instructions and measurements are useful for paper sizes 4" square and larger.

1. Place the paper in front of you, horizontally (if it is a rectangle).
2. Fold the paper in half widthwise. Open.
3. Measure and mark $1^1/2$" from the edge of the top long side. This will be the top of your page. To make it easier to fold, you can score a line here.
4. Fold at the score across the top. Open.
5. Measure and mark $1/4$" on either side of the middle fold.
6. Fold in the ends to these marks, each end to the mark closest to it. Open.
7. With your scissors or knife, cut out the top right and left rectangles (or squares). Leave the two top middle sections intact.
8. Diagonally fold down each of the four corners of the main part of the paper, aligning the vertical edges just before the vertical folds. Keep these folded.
9. Fold the edges over again, this time to the middle pencil marks.
10. Turn the paper over, keeping everything folded.

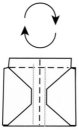

steps 9 and 10

step 11   step 12

step 13

11. Fold up the bottom to align with the top fold. The top tab will protrude.

12. Fold the top tab over the page and tuck it into the pockets at the edges.

13. Fold the page in half widthwise.

14. Repeat steps 1-13 for all pages.

Assembling the book:

15. Keep the pages folded. Measure and mark $1/2$" from the head and tail on the spines of all the pages.

16. For half the pages, make marks on the spines, centered between the other two marks.

17. For the pages with only two marks, make narrow diagonal cuts (triangles) at the head and tail, with the point just above $1/32$") the mark and the wide part at the edge of the paper.

18. For the pages with the third mark, cut a narrow diamond shape, with the top and bottom points at the marks and the middle point just to the right or left ($1/8$" to $1/4$") of the middle mark.

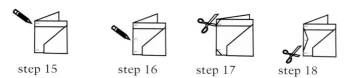

step 15   step 16   step 17   step 18

19. Set aside the pages in pairs with one triangular page and one diamond page in each pair.

20. Pick up one pair of pages. Keep the diamond page closed. Open the triangular page.

21. Lightly bend/fold in the corners on the right side or curl the pages up to make a loose circle.

22. With one hand, hold onto the overlapping corners.

23. Tuck this triangular roll through the diamond hole in the diamond page.

step 19

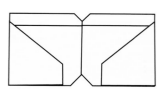

step 20

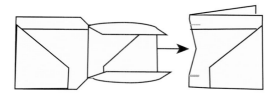

steps 21, 22, and 23

24. Pull through gently. Uncurl the triangular page and smooth it flat.

25. Repeat steps 20-24 for the other pairs of pages.

26. Arrange the pairs so that the diamond hole is visible. Make sure the pockets are all at the bottom. The diamond hole pages will have the fold/spine on the right as you work.

27. Do steps 20-24 again, this time joining the triangular front page of one pair with the diamond back page of the previous pair.

28. Slip a piece of museum board into each of the open sections at the front and back fore edge. Trim the boards to fit, if necessary. Remove the boards.

29. Fold the four strips of paper lengthwise.

30. Apply glue or glue stick to the back of one 2" wide strip. Wrap the strip around one edge of one board and press down. Apply glue to a second strip and press into place across from the first strip. These strips will be parallel to the spine.

31. Repeat step 30 for the remaining three boards.

32. Slip the boards back into place in the open sections, with the strips at the fore edge.

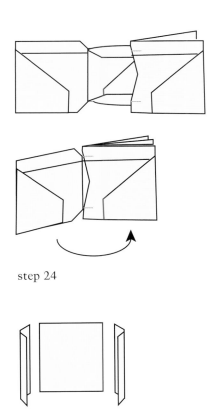

step 24

steps 29 and 30

Greetings, 2000; greeting cards; unique; 5¹/₄" x 7¹/₄" x ³/₄"

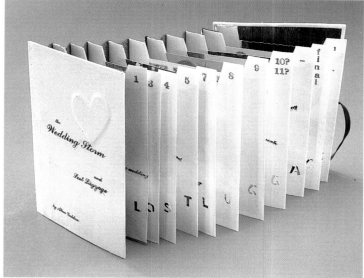

Left: *Photos*, 2000; handmade envelope pages, photographs; unique;
5" x 6¹/₂" x ³/₄" depth
Right: *The Wedding Storm and Lost
Luggage*, 2000; envelopes, postcards,
iron-on transfers; unique;
5" x 6³/₄" x 1"

POCKET FRAME BOOK
(FOLDING, CUTTING, GLUING)

The Wedding Storm and Lost Luggage contains commercially made
envelopes. *Photos*, which is this pocket frame book, contains handmade
envelope pages with windows. I left a margin at the top of each page for a
caption. For the following example you will have a ¹/₂" top margin.

Tools: ruler, pencil, scissors or art knife and cutting mat, glue or glue stick
Materials: Seven sheets heavyweight paper 13¹/₂" x 5⁵/₈", grained long, one
sheet medium-weight paper 12" x 7", grained short

1. Fold the 12" x 7" paper into an accordion with sixteen segments (see
page 140).
2. Put one sheet of the heavyweight paper in front of you, oriented
vertically.
3. Measure and mark ³/₄" from the right and left edges.
4. Score lines vertically at these two places.
5. Measure and mark 6¹/₂" from the top.
6. Score a horizontal line at this mark.
7. Starting at the left edge, cut a slit along the horizontal line, stopping at
the vertical score (the slit will be ³/₄").
8. On the right-hand side, cut off the top right rectangle. (Leave the bottom
right rectangle.)
9. Measure and mark a window in the bottom panel, leaving at least a ³/₄"
margin of paper all the way around.

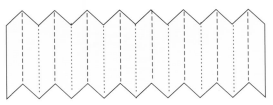

step 1

step 3

steps 7 and 8

step 10

step 13

10. Using an art knife, cut out this window.

11. Valley-fold along the bottom right and left rectangles. Open.

12. Apply a thin line of glue to cover these two rectangles. They are flaps.

13. Keeping the two flaps folded, fold the paper in half widthwise, along the horizontal score.

14. Press and smooth down the glued tabs. This is a frame. You will notice a third tab sticking out on the left.

15. Repeat steps 2-14 for the other six pieces of paper.

16. Arrange the accordion-folded paper in front of you with a valley fold as the first fold on the left.

17. Adhere the pages from back to front. Apply a thin, flat line of glue to the segment of the accordion that is just to the right of the second-to-last valley fold. Keep the very last valley fold unglued.

18. Press down the tab of one of your frames onto the accordion, making sure you align it with the fold.

19. Repeat steps 17 and 18 for the other six frames, each time gluing to the segment just after a valley fold. Try to align each frame with the previous frame as you go.

20. Add two 7 1/4" x 5" glued separate hard covers (see page 148), or two 7" x 4⁷/8" wrapped hard covers (see page 140).

Note: if you want more pages/frames, make two accordion-fold spines. The first accordion should have a valley fold for its first fold; the second should be oriented with a peak fold as its first fold. Glue the accordion-fold spines together. You will have to cut off the last segment of the last accordion.

Julie Chen: *Leavings*, 1995; letterpress printed from photopolymer plates on a variety of papers; edition of 100 copies; closed: 4¹/4" x 6¹/2" open: 51" (length). Box: 7" x 5" x 1⁵/8"

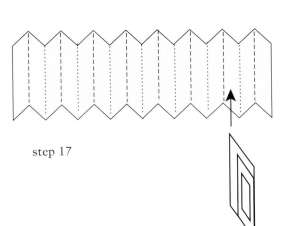

step 17

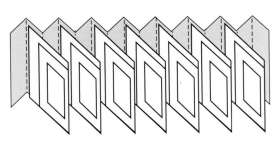

step 19

STOCK BOOK
(FOLDING, CUTTING, GLUING, SEWING)

Stamp collectors use a book with narrow glassine pockets to store the stamps they have collected before they go into the stamp album. The book, called a *stock book*, keeps the stamps dry and flat until they are transferred to the stamp album. The glassine is acid free and therefore will not transfer any yellow spots to the stamps. When you purchase postage stamps, save the glassine bags. Cut the bags and use them for the pocket strips for this project. Or buy glassine in a large sheet from an art supply store. Glassine sheets are often placed between drawings or other artwork to be stored. All papers are grained short unless otherwise indicated.

Tools: needle, awl or leather punch, cardboard to protect work surface, cutting mat, scissors, pencil, glue or glue stick

Materials: For the pages: twelve 2" x 9" glassine strips grained long, $64^1/2$" self-adhesive linen tape, three 7" x 9" 2-ply boards, three 7" x $1^1/8$" 2-ply board spine strips grained long, two 7" x 10" glassine pages, two 7" x 10" end papers. **For the covers:** two $7^1/4$" x 10" 4-ply boards, two $7^1/4$" x 1" 4-ply board spine strips, grained long, two 13" x $9^1/4$" cover papers, two $10^3/4$" x 7" inner cover papers, 14" of ribbon or heavy thread
Example: $7^1/4$" x 10" book

1. Fold all glassine strips lengthwise.
2. Apply a thin line of glue or glue stick to the inside of the open edge. Press down.
3. Place the three 7" x 9" boards horizontally in front of you. Measure and make light pencil lines every $1^3/4$ inches.
4. Put a thin line of glue on one of the pencil lines. Align a glassine strip with the newly glued edge pointed down. You are making a long, thin pocket with the folded edge as the opening of the pocket.
5. Repeat step 4 for all pencil lines.
6. Align one $1^1/8$" x 7" board strip with a board page, leaving a gap of $3/16$".
7. Place an 8" strip of self-adhesive linen tape across the gap, and wrap it around the edges.

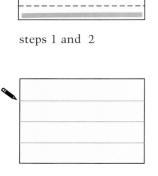

steps 1 and 2

step 3

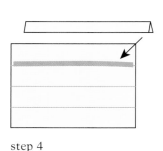

step 4

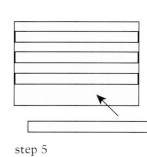

step 5

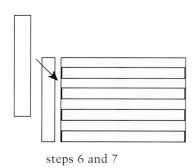

steps 6 and 7

Priority Mail, 2000; manila envelopes, glassine, stamps, hand-written text; unique; 10" x 7"

8. Turn the page over. Place a 6 ¹/₂" strip of the self-adhesive linen tape on the back across the gap.

9. Take a 7" piece of linen tape or a decorative paper strip and wrap it around the fore edge. This will secure the glassine strips.

10. Repeat steps 2-9 for all the board pages.

For the cover:

11. Arrange the cover paper in front of you horizontally, wrong-side up.

12. On the cover paper place one board and one strip with ¹/₄" between them. Leave a one-inch margin around the edges.

13. With a pencil, draw lines around the board and board strip. Remove the boards.

14. Apply glue to the paper. Align the boards and press down.

15. Turn over the project and smooth down the paper onto the boards.

16. Turn it back over. Cut off the corners with scissors, leaving approximately ¹/₈" space between the paper you cut off and the board.

17. Spread glue on each of the flaps and turn them in, one by one. After gluing one or two flaps, or if your scrap paper gets messy, get new scrap paper and continue gluing.

18. Smooth down all paper.

19. Spread glue on the wrong side of one of the inner cover papers.

20. Center it and smooth it down on the back of the boards just covered.

21. Place the covered boards between two sheets of waxed paper and put under a heavy book.

22. Repeat steps 11-21 for the second cover.

23. Let the boards dry for 1-5 days under the heavy book before assembling the stock book.

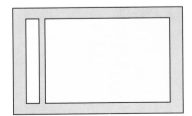

step 8

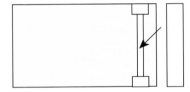

step 9

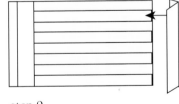

step 12

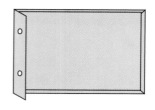

step 25

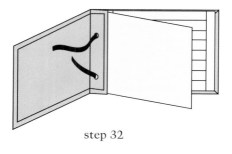

step 32

Assembling the book:

24. Measure $1/2$" from one edge of each of the cover strips. Measure $1^1/2$" from the head and tail. Poke or punch holes in the strips at the intersection of these marks.

25. Take the back cover and bend the strip of board to the inside. The strip will be on the left.

26. Align the left edge of the back cover with the left edge of each of the inner pages. Keep the inner pages flat.

27. Turn the front cover wrong-side up so that the strip is on the right. Align it with the inner pages so that when the cover is closed the front and back covers will be aligned.

28. With a pencil, draw around the inside of the punched holes of the cover strip onto one of the inner pages, glassine pages, and endsheets.

29. Use the cover for a template and draw circles on all the inner pages.

30. Punch or poke the holes in the pages.

31. Stack the inner pages neatly with the endpapers, front and back, and the glassine pages between them.

32. Using approximately 12" of ribbon or heavy thread, sew from front to back through the holes.

33. Tie the ends of ribbon together in a square knot. Then make a bow and another square knot, if desired.

Note: You may substitute two screw posts for the ribbon. Look for these in a bookbinding supply, stationery, or hardware store. They may be made of plastic, aluminum, or brass. If you use the posts you can easily add pages to your stock book. The posts fit holes the size of standard office hole punches.

STAMP WALLET
(FOLDING, SLITTING, GLUING)

This stamp wallet was found among some old family papers. Its origin is mysterious. I adapted it so I could make one. For more details on how to cover the boards, see Materials and Methods: Covers and Dust Jackets, page 148.

Tools: pencil, art knife, metal ruler, cutting mat, PVA, glue brush, magazines for scrap paper, white plastic eraser, bone folder

Materials: Two pieces of 4-ply museum board, $4^1/2$" x $6^1/2$", grained long, one sheet of cover paper, $6^1/2$" x $8^1/2$", grained short, one spine strip, $6^1/2$" x 1", grained long, two medium- to heavy-weight endsheets 4" x 6", grained long, six strips of heavy Mylar, 2" x $3^1/2$"

1. Place one of the endsheets in front of you, vertically oriented.
2. Measure and mark $3/4$" from the top.
3. Measure and mark 1" from the first mark and from each successive mark. You should have six marks when you get to the bottom of the endsheet.

4. Measure $1/2$" from the right and left edges. Draw two vertical lines.

5. With an art knife against a ruler, cut horizontal slits (between the vertical lines) at the second, fourth, and sixth horizontal lines. Cut vertical slits connecting horizontal lines 1 and 2, 3 and 4, 5 and 6. (See diagram.) You are creating flaps that look like long, squared-off "U" shapes.

6. Repeat steps 1-5 for the second endsheet.

7. Fold each of the six Mylar strips in half lengthwise. Crease well with the bone folder.

8. Turn over one endsheet.

9. Take one flap of the endsheet and bend it up slightly. Sandwich the flap betwen the folds of the Mylar.

10. Apply a dot of PVA to the right and left edges of the Mylar. Slip the ends through the slits and press them to the back of the endsheet.

11. Repeat steps 8-10 for all six pieces of Mylar.

12. Cover the boards with one piece of paper, leaving a $5/8$" gap at the spine.

13. Put a thin, even coat of PVA on the spine strip and adhere it across the gap.

14. Put an even coat of PVA on one endsheet, turn it over and adhere the endsheet to the covered boards.

15. Repeat for remaining endsheet.

16. With a white plastic eraser, erase the pencil lines on the endsheets. Don't use a pink one, it will leave smudges.

17. Put waxed paper in the center and let the wallet dry overnight under heavy weights.

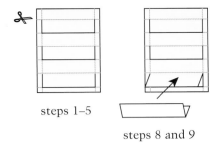

steps 1–5

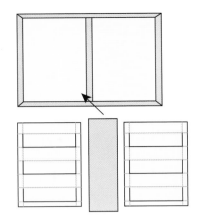

steps 8 and 9

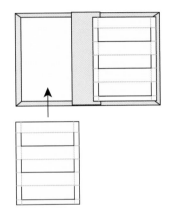

step 13

Left: *Stamp Wallet*, date unknown; $4^1/2$" x $6^3/4$"
Right: *Stamp Wallet*, 2000; acrylic-painted endsheets, Mylar; unique; $4\ ^1/4$" x 6"

CHAPTER 4

THICK SEWN BOOKS

When you create a book with many pages, you need to think about how much time you want the reader to spend on each page. How much information you put on a page will control the pacing. A detailed collage or lots of text will cause the reader to stop and examine it. Conversely, a simple block of solid color or a single word will cause the reader to move on rapidly. A book will be read slowly or not at all if it contains only heavily detailed pages. A book with all simple pages will be read quickly. Think about balancing detailed pages with simple pages.

You can also vary the reading experience by adding the unexpected. Marie Dern finds a place for three-dimensional objects in some of her books. The books begin with a text, as you might expect, but eventually you turn the page and find a three-dimensional object cradled in a hole. Marie combines surprise and humor with the seriousness of the text. By isolating an object within a book you cause the reader to stop and think about its meaning and importance.

Marie Dern: *Peaches,* 1993; steel covers with copper patina; watercolor painting by Carl Dern, Coptic binding; unique; 6^1/$_2$" x 9^1/$_2$" x ^{3}/$_4$" (photo by C. Dern)

"For many years I've put things away in books: letters, flowers, mementos of one kind or another, only to find them months, or even years, later. I like the surprise of finding something between the pages of a book. It is no doubt in the natural course of things that I began to put things in the books I make. The very shape of a book suggests a box, so I began cutting out the insides of books and putting things inside. This led to making the books from scratch, designed to be hollowed out. I've made many of these over the years. A template for the hole is placed over the sections and cut; then the book is sewn with the section placed exactly one on top of the other so the hole remains. It is fairly important to sew tight so there is not too much play in the spine. The pages with the holes are then glued to each other and to the back cover, so that it becomes a solid block.

Marie Dern: *Peaches*, open to gun made by Carl Dern (photo by C. Dern)

"*Peaches* is a story I wrote about my grandmother and me being held at gunpoint when I was a child. There's a gun (made of steel by Carl Dern) hidden beneath the pages of the story. I tried to buy a handgun at a pawn shop. I told the salesman I wanted one that didn't work and explained I was putting it inside a book. I could tell by his face he knew I was a lunatic. He said that he only had guns that worked and wasn't about to sell me one anyway. The gun Carl made is much better, so it all worked out.

"*L'Oeuf dans le Livre* is another book of this kind. There is no text: just a title page, then a page with a chicken printed in yellow, and then the page is turned and there's an egg in a little nest. I was inspired by the incongruity of the reader finding a tiny egg in a nest of flowers in a book with a printed title page. The title *L'Oeuf dans le Livre* is in French because I love the sound of l'oeuf, luff."

MARIE C. DERN

Marie Dern: *L'Oeuf dans le Livre*, 1992; letterpress, hosho text paper, pastegrain covers over museum board, quail's egg, flowers; chain stich binding; 5^3/$_4$" x 4^3/$_8$" x 1^1/$_4$" (photo by C. Dern)

Woven House Book, 2000;
paper, museum board, watercolor
pencil, waxed linen; unique;
$3^1/4$" x $3^1/2$" x $^3/4$"

DECORATIVE STITCH BOOK WITH WEAVING

This structure works well if you use a decorated paper around each of the signatures since you will see the decorated paper from the outside. Use an odd number of signatures; five works well. You will do the weaving last, after the books are sewn together.

Tools: pencil, ruler, needle, two colors of waxed macrame thread, bone folder, knife, cutting mat
Materials: For the outer paper of each of the five signatures: five different decorated papers, each $5^1/2$" x $8^1/2$", grained short. **For the inner pages:** twenty sheets of $5^1/2$" x $8 ^1/2$" lightweight paper, grained short

1. Fold all the pages in half widthwise.
2. Nest four of the lighter-weight papers inside one of the decorated papers.
3. Repeat for each of the decorated papers. You should now have five signatures, or five sets of five pages.
4. Measure and mark $^1/2$" from the head and tail of one of the signatures. Also measure $1^1/2$" from the head and tail, and mark it. Use this signature as a guide to make similar marks on the other four signatures.

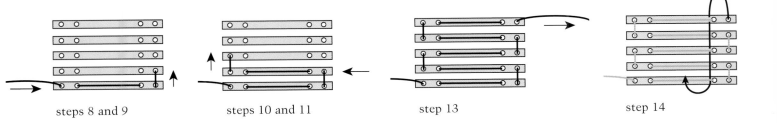

steps 8 and 9   steps 10 and 11   step 13   step 14

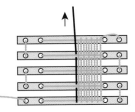

step 15

5. Keeping the signatures folded, rest each of the signatures on top of each other and align the spines. The marks should be aligned as well.

6. Make a notch with your knife through all the signatures at the marks, or poke holes with your needle.

7. Take a length of thread that is approximately 25" long. Do not knot it.

8. Leave 9" of thread. Start at the head and sew a running stitch to the tail of the book from inside to outside. You will end outside.

9. Sew from the outside of this signature to the outside of the next signature.

10. Sew a running stitch to the head of the book.

11. Add the third signature and continue the running stitch.

12. Add the fourth signature and continue the running stitch.

13. Add the fifth signature and finish the running stitch.

14. Begin the weaving by going over and under the exposed stitches.

15. Take the thread off the needle when you have about 2" to spare and have finished a row.

16. Rethread the needle with the 9" trail of thread from the beginning of the first signature and weave with this piece. The first weaving pattern should match the weaving pattern of the other side that is going in the opposite direction.

17. When you get to 2" of thread from this second piece, make sure that the two tails of thread are at the same end of the row. Tie the two ends together in a square knot. Tie in a bow, if you like, then tie in another knot to secure the bow.

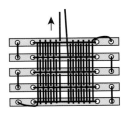

step 17

To secure the head and tail of the book:

18. Rethread the needle with another color of thread.

19. Leave a tail of thread that is about 2" long.

20. Take the thread from inside to outside in a hole at the tail of the book.

21. Take your needle from side to side under each of the exposed threads at the head of the book. (See diagram.)

22. Come back down the signatures.

23. Tie off the ends.

24. Repeat for the head of the book.

25. Adhere separate $5^{1}/2$" x $4^{1}/4$" 4-ply boards to the front and back end papers (like bread on a sandwich). See page 148 if you wish to cover the boards first.

26. Wrap in waxed paper and put under weights to dry overnight.

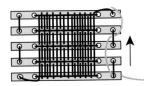

step 17

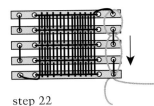

steps 18–21

step 22

Left: Catherine Michaelis: *Book: A Cherokee Primer*, 1993; letterpress; edition of 100; 4 × 5³/₄"
Right: Catherine Michaelis: *Book: A Cherokee Primer*, open

EXPOSED STITCH BOOK WITH BEADS

I purchased a copy of Catherine Michaelis's *Book: A Cherokee Primer* because the materials she used intrigued me: I liked the bark paper and the turquoise-colored beads. I had never seen the beaded spine before and set out to make a model of it. It was harder than I thought. I found that I had to thread and unthread the needle several times. When you practice this binding, pick a time when you feel calm and unhurried. The finished product will be worth the effort.

"Book: A Cherokee Primer was my first May Day Press publication. I printed it in honor of my part-Cherokee grandmother for all that she taught me. The way she lived her life inspires me and brings me comfort. I find it difficult to put my feelings about her into words: perhaps that is why I continue to make pieces about her and for her. The text contains words of nature: butterfly, flower, hummingbird, sun, and lists both the English and Cherokee, with linoleum-cut illustrations for each page, much as a child's schoolbook would. I chose Mexican bark paper and the exposed stitched binding to give it a very raw, handmade quality. I wanted it to evoke a book made by someone with few materials and limited skills (like me) but in an older era."
CATHERINE MICHAELIS

Tools: pencil, ruler, needle, thread, bone folder, knife, cutting mat

Materials: For the cover: $5^3/4$" x 15" heavy paper. The cover or wrapper should be the width of your pages opened, plus the depth of the signatures stacked up (in this example, four signatures stacked should measure approximately $1/2$"). You will also have edge flaps that will be folded in (3" in this example).

For the text or inner paper: sixteen papers, $5^1/2$" x $8^1/2$", grained short.

1. Fold all text pages in half.
2. Nest four sheets inside one another to make signatures.
3. Stack up signatures. Measure this depth (it should be about $1/2$").
4. Place the cover paper in front of you horizontally oriented.
5. Find the middle of your cover paper (don't fold, just lightly mark with a pencil). Measure and mark $1/4$" on each side of your tiny midline pencil; mark both head and tail.
6. Score a vertical line with your thumbnail or bone folder and ruler.
7. From both sides of the score line, measure the width of your book (in our example, $4^1/4$"). Mark and score.
8. Fold in the edge flaps.

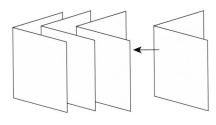

steps 1 and 2

step 3

To sew:

The middle bead is sewn in line with the rest of the stitching, horizontally (when the book is being sewn). The end beads are sewn vertically, to the next signature. For this binding you will make eight sets of four holes (these will be your sewing stations) along the spine of your wrapper (soft cover). On the inside of the wrapper so the marks will not show, mark lines across where the holes will go.

9. Measure $1/2$" from the head and tail. Mark these two places.
10. Measure and mark 1" from the head and tail.
11. Measure and mark 2" from the head and tail.
12. Measure and mark $2^3/4$" from the head and tail.
13. Use a ruler and measure four vertical guidelines in the center; your light mark at the midline will be one of the lines, the other two vertical marks at the spine will be the second and third. Measure $1/8$" between the midline mark and the outer marks to make the fourth and fifth lines.
14. With a needle, poke four holes, centered between each line.
15. With signatures stacked and spines facing you, using the wrapper as a guide, draw lines or mark on the signatures exactly where the holes will be on the signatures.

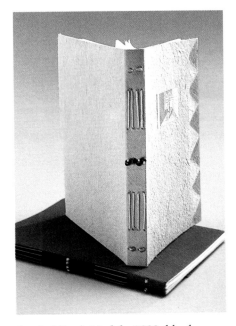

Beaded Book Models, 2000; blank; $4^1/4$" x $5^3/4$"

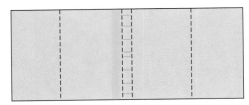

steps 5–13

step 14

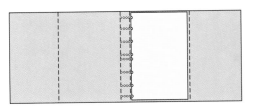

steps 15, 16, and 17

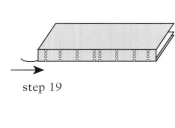

step 19

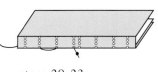

steps 20–23

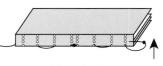

steps 28 and 29

steps 30 and 31

step 31

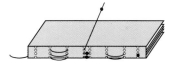  

step 32

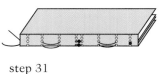

steps 33 and 34

step 35

steps 36 and 37

16. You may use an art knife to cut notches at these marks or an awl or needle to make holes in each signature separately.

17. Stack signatures inside the wrapper, holes aligned with wrapper. Keeping the same orientation, remove the signatures and place them in front of you.

18. Place the wrapper with the spine facing you, the fore edge away from you. Start by placing the bottom signature inside the wrapper.

19. Use about an arm's length of thread, or four to five times the length of the book. Begin sewing by taking the thread from the outside of the signature at the end to the inside of the signature.

20. Come back out, sewing through the wrapper as well.

21. Sew from outside to inside.

22. Sew inside to outside.

23. Take your needle off and thread one of the center beads onto the thread.

24. Rethread the needle and sew from outside to inside.

25. Sew from inside to outside.

26. Sew from outside to inside.

27. Sew from inside to outside.

28. Remove your needle. (Poke it into cork or pin cushion briefly so you don't lose it.) Thread one of the tail beads onto the thread.

29. Sew into the second set of holes from outside to inside.

30. Continue the running stitch, in and out until you get to the center, where you will add the bead.

31. Thread the bead and keep going until you get to the head of the book. Don't sew through the wrapper at the head of the book.

32. Continue sewing and adding beads, leaving the holes at the head of the book's wrapper empty until the very last signature.

33. When all four signatures are sewn to the wrapper, come out the hole at the head of the book through the wrapper.

34. Add one bead, rethread the needle, and sew into the wrapper only.

35. Come back out the wrapper and add the second bead.

36. Go back inside the wrapper only.

37. Find the first end, pull it around to the last end; tie the ends in a square knot inside the wrapper.

BOOK ON STICKS

Use a decorated paper around each of the five signatures since they will be visible from the outside of the book.

Tools: pencil, ruler, needle, heavy thread such as waxed macramé thread, bone folder, knife, cutting mat

Materials: For the outer paper of each of the five signatures: five different decorated papers, each $5^1/2$" x $8^1/2$", grained short. **For the inner pages:** twenty sheets of $5^1/2$" x $8^1/2$" lightweight paper, grained short, five straight sticks (approximately $1/8$"–$1/4$" in diameter)

1. Fold all the pages in half widthwise.
2. Nest four of the lighter-weight papers inside one of the decorated papers.
3. Repeat for each of the decorated papers. You should now have five signatures, or five sets of five pages.
4. Measure and mark $3/4$" from the head and tail of one of the signatures. Also measure $2^3/4$" from the head and mark it. (This mark should be the center.) Use this signature as a guide to make similar marks on the other four signatures.
5. Keeping the signatures folded, rest each of the signatures on top of each other and align the spines. The marks should be aligned as well.
6. Make a notch with your knife through all the signatures at the marks, or poke holes with your needle.
7. Take a length of thread that is approximately 25" long. Do not knot it.

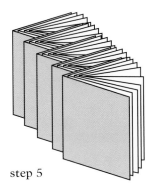

step 5

step 6

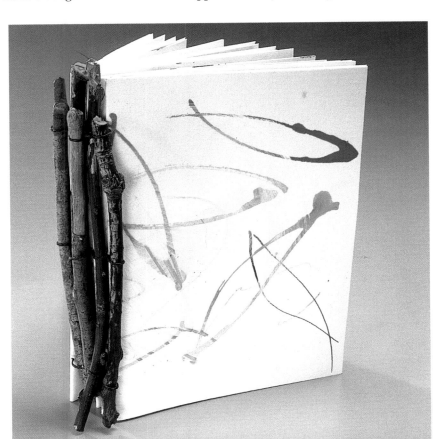

Stick Book Model, 2000; sticks, paper; unique; $4^3/4$" x $5^3/4$"

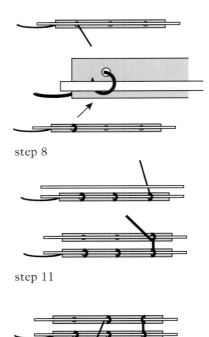

step 8

step 11

step 12

8. Start on the inside of the first signature and sew from inside to outside. Make a loop around one stick and sew back into the same hole. Tie a square knot with the tail and the rest of the thread. Do not cut.

9. Sew to the middle hole from inside to outside. Make a loop around the stick and sew back into the same middle hole.

10. Sew to the last hole from inside to outside. Make a loop around the stick and sew back into the same last hole. Tie a knot to the stitches inside. Do not cut the thread.

11. Come back out the same last hole. Put the second stick on top of the working thread and close to the first stick. Wrap thread over the second stick and sew into the second signature from outside to inside.

12. Sew to the middle hole of the second signature from inside to outside.

13. When you come out of the middle hole, take your thread up between the two sticks. Go over then under the second stick. Go through the stitch of the preceding stick. Now go back under the new stick into the same middle hole. You are making a single stitch around each stick.

14. Repeat step 13 for the third hole.

15. At the end of that signature, tie a knot to the stitches inside. Come back out the same hole to add the next signature.

16. Repeat steps 11–15 for all the signatures and sticks.

step 13

step 14

step 16

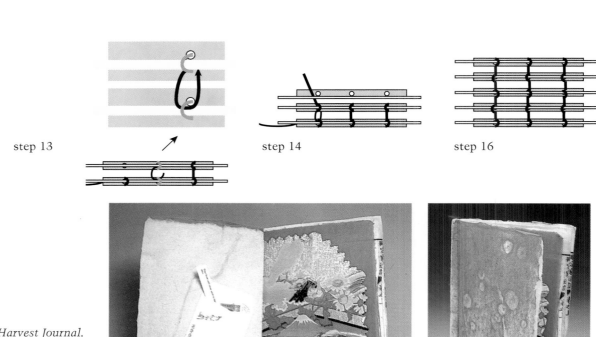

Left: Val Simonetti: *Harvest Journal*, 1982; open
Right: Val Simonetti: *Harvest Journal*, 1982; handmade and store-bought papers, found materials, letterpress, handwritten text, letters; 6" x 9"

CHAPTER 5

TRANSFORMING EVERYDAY LIFE

The French Symbolist poet Stéphane Mallarmé had the idea that everything in the world existed to become a book. We can extend this idea and say that everything in the world exists to become book *art*.

Throughout history, each culture has made books with available materials. In the Tigris-Euphrates valley, people inscribed the clay that was abundant there and baked it into a variety of shapes. Although these forms had pictographic stories, they were not "book shaped" as we now know the book; they were cones, columns, and circles. In India, people wrote on palm leaves. In Egypt, they wrote on paper made from the papyrus plant as well as on animal hides, and stitched the sheets together to make long scrolls. The Greeks and Romans made thick wooden frames, filled them with wax, and bound them together at the edge to make their first books. The word *codex*, the modern-day book, comes from *caudex*, from the Latin for tree trunk, board, or writing tablet.

Left: Lisa Kokin: *Sometimes a Great Notion,* 1992; text by the artist, mixed-media sewing notions, fabric, sewing patterns; 6" x 5" x 1" (photo by L. Kokin)
Right: Lisa Kokin: *Sometimes a Great Notion* (detail)

Although paper is common in our culture and used extensively for bookmaking, we continue to seek other materials to make books and art. Kurt Schwitters, an anti-Nazi artist who left Germany for England in the 1940s, found lodging near the Thames and picked out wrappers and driftwood from the river to create collages and assemblages. In 1992, Berkeley-based artist Lisa Kokin used old sewing patterns in her book titled (after a book by Ken Kesey) *Sometimes a Great Notion.* Lisa's book begins "Textiles are a genetic condition with me." Cloth is a prominent part

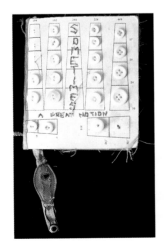
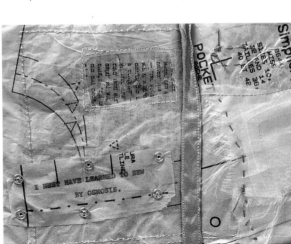

of her family's history, beginning with her Romanian immigrant grandmother who worked in a tie factory in the early 1900s. Growing up in her parents' small upholstery shop further influenced Lisa as she made collages out of left-over pieces of Naugahyde, vinyl, and foam rubber. In her current one-of-a-kind books, Lisa uses photographs, plastic objects, old books, and other things gleaned from flea markets. You will bring your own personality and back-ground to your work by using materials familiar and important to *you*.

ALTERED BOOKS
(CUTTING, GLUING)

There is a collaborator out there waiting for you. You don't have to get along. You probably won't ever meet. He or she is the author of an already published book, perhaps a third edition or damaged reprint of no monetary value. Here is a theme, perhaps a collection of characters or theories. Someone has started your project for you; you are not faced with a blank page.

For three and sixpence, Tom Phillips bought a book published in 1892 called *A Human Document,* by William Hurrell Mallock. In 1966 Phillips began altering the book. Inspired by William Burroughs's technique of cutting up writing and rearranging text, Phillips began painting out and over much of the text of the old book, leaving only certain phrases made up of the text found there. The altered book, which he called *A Humument,* was first pub-lished by a commercial press in 1980 in a mass-market edition. Tom Phillips writes an acknowledgment to W.H. Mallock, his "unwitting collaborator."

Content is suggested; theme is waiting to be discovered. If you live near a used bookstore, ask if they have a box of books they are going to throw away. Many times a book just needs a few repairs but is currently unsalable, so it

Left: Lisa Kokin: *A Guide to Painting,* 1999; mixed media, altered book; 5³/4" x 3" x 3" (photo by J.W. White, courtesy of Catharine Clark Gallery, San Francisco)
Right: Lisa Kokin: *A Guide to Painting* (detail)

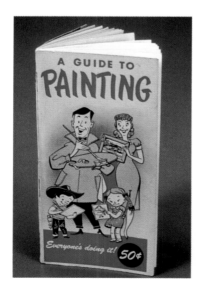

Lisa Kokin: *Things and Situations*, 1999; mixed media, altered book; 4¼" x 1¾" x 1¾" (photo by J.W. White, courtesy of Catharine Clark Gallery, San Francisco)

gets discarded; you might get a book that was headed for the landfill, so you need not feel guilty revising it. Go to a garage sale and get old textbooks or other dry material that you can embellish.

Altering a book is another way of working with found material. Lisa Kokin uses thin strips of shredded money to block out lines of text. Sometimes she collages images on top of the pages, such as what she did for the old 1950s book called *A Guide to Painting*. She also stitches over lines of text and provocatively chops books into thin slices.

"As greed and intolerance consume the planet, I sit in my studio cutting up, rearranging, and rewriting books to make them say what I believe to be true. Humor is essential. Laughing in the face of despair is an old Jewish trick; it worked for the folks back in the Old Country and it works for me.

"I have always been fascinated by the sounds and meanings of words —puns and double-entendres make me ecstatic. When I was a kid I used to spend hours on the phone with my friends playing a game called *Mad Libs*, a booklet of short vignettes with different parts of speech omitted. The kid who had the story in front of her would ask the other to name a noun, verb, or adjective at random until all the spaces were filled in. Then she would read back the story with strange and inappropriate words, which caused it to veer off into surreal territory, and we'd laugh ourselves silly.

"Recently, I realized that I'm playing a sort of *Mad Libs* with myself in my new work. Cutting up text from wildly different sources and then pasting it together in a sort of literary assemblage, I am doing with words what I also do with objects. I like the odd juxtapositions—religious text with phrases from *Fortune* magazine, a marriage manual with a guide to hunting game, and so on.

"I grew up in a house filled with books which were treated with utmost reverence. Cutting them up will probably land me in hell eventually, but at least I'm having fun."

LISA KOKIN

MEMORY JOGS

In January 2000 I went to an exhibit of bookworks by Anne Hicks Siberell. A large body of the work incorporated small wooden boxes that housed cast concrete, into which Anne had placed bits of found materials: photographs, tickets, ribbons, cloth, credit card imprints. The most intriguing pieces to me had a piece of vellum with writing on it placed next to an open box. The writing, while not descriptive of the actual objects embedded in the concrete, tied the objects together by providing a mood or a place. The concrete tablets with the objects took on new importance with the anecdote placed beside them. They weren't just stuff anymore. They had a story and a meaning.

After the show I began to wonder whether the bits of ephemera stuck into the concrete were things that Anne already had in her house or studio for many years, or whether she had been on the lookout for interesting objects. Were her pieces nonfiction or fiction? The writing felt biographical. If these were objects that she already had in her desk or at the bottom of her bag, then I imagined all the work to be very personal or nonfictional. This would be the stuff of everyday life without self-consciousness. Nonfiction is the truth, and fiction is consciously invented.

But an invented story can be very powerful. Had Anne been hunting for things, gleaning from the world, picking and choosing, making a conscious decision as to what is interesting or unusual and then collecting them to use later? The fiction is in creating a piece from objects that do not belong to you (not your bus transfer or program cover or cloth from your own clothes), they haven't been at the bottom of your desk for decades. They don't tell a story about *you*. But in fiction, unlike nonfiction, you can create a story that may

Anne Hicks Siberell: *The Day Before Yesterday's Ancient Tablets: ARCHEOLOGY*, 1980s–present; cement, wood, mixed media; 8" x 6" x 1 1/2" (photo by Gary Sinick)

say more precisely what you want to communicate. Maybe you don't own a piece of cloth that really says "romance" or "roughness" and that piece of cloth is important in communicating your story.

Instead of guessing about Anne's work any further, I decided to call her. She said that she was a pack rat. Her house was built before there was a regular garbage pickup service so that the backyard was rather like a dump. She found shards of all kinds of things. Her kids found old toys. She told me she assembles objects that remind her of personal stories. Anne has done much research on storytelling in different cultures. The boxes are reminiscent of these.

Anne Hicks Siberell: *The Day Before Yesterday's Ancient Tablets: WE'D MEET AT THE MET*, 1980s–present; cement, wood, mixed media; 8" × 6" × 2" (photo by Gary Sinick)

 "People who make visual art do a little every day. Writers write every day. I write but I don't always write everything down and I don't write every day. The objects are like reminders of the stories I want to remember.

"In my work I have used forms of Mesopotamian tablets, Native American scrolls, Aboriginal message sticks, and ancient Roman *volumen* or rolls. After illustrating books about various Native American Indian tribes with woodcuts, I began studying ways of communicating among people with no written language. The Ojibwa Indians recorded stories, songs, and ways of healing through pictographs carved into bark. Since these memory-jogging notations were derived from an individual carver's personal sense of symbolism, the meaning of each scroll could be read and understood only by its maker. Likewise, much in my pieces can only be 'my story'; however, many of the symbols used are universal and meant to trigger a memory in the viewer's mind as well.

"I used to keep journals in blank books. As a child I wrote but later liberally censored my five-year diary, confiding 'Dear Diary, YOU know what happened...' Now, decades later, the diary tells me nothing. As an adult I found myself still reluctant to write anything but the decorous in my journals—heaven forbid someone should read it. I began to make collaged diaries in accordion-fold books, in which primarily visual material flowed from panel to panel to tell a story. I find that pictures trigger memory in a different way.

"While researching the origin of Babylonian clay tablets for a book I was writing for children, I came across an explanation of the origin of writing. The explanation inspired me to study the complicated systems of marks of the first written languages. It occurred to me that tablets like the Babylonian tablets might work for my diaries. Symbols and souvenirs form a kind of language, signaling memory. By using wet concrete I can mold and paint, add objects, wait for the materials to dry, then paint, draw, or carve on the solid surface. After the tablets are finished I make wood boxes to house them so I can stack or send them out more securely.

Anne Hicks Siberell: *The Day Before Yesterday's Ancient Tablets: BEIRUT*, 1980s–present; cement, wood, mixed media; 8" × 6" × 2" (photo by Gary Sinick)

"*The Day Before Yesterday's Ancient Tablets* are made up of Vol. I and Vol. II. The first set is a smaller tablet. I placed them in hand-sewn vinyl envelopes for storage. When I began Vol. II I used 9-ply birch bark for base and cover, and wood bought in hobby shops for making model airplanes for sides. I glued it together with white glue. Then I came across a retired woodworker who seemed to enjoy making boxes. He mostly made the smaller ones, replacing the vinyl envelopes. So far, I guess there are several hundred tablets.

"Some of the tablets are accompanied by text on vellum; however, these words don't always explain what the tablets represent. Other tablets are without text. I like that information can be recorded, stored, then brought into focus without what we recognize as our traditional written language."

ANNE HICKS SIBERELL

When you create a bookwork, you may wish to present a story (in words or images or both) as close to the truth as you can. This may be for a record of an event or for posterity. Or you may want a stronger or different flavor and mood by consciously altering what actually happened.

SPIRAL BINDING
(PUNCHING, WINDING WIRE)

This book has a homey, handmade look to it. If you wish your binding to look perfect, purchase a commercially made spiral-bound book from an art-supply or office-supply store.

A punch is better than an awl for this project since it removes the excess paper, allowing the wire to move more freely in the hole. I found a rotating leather punch at a hardware store; on its rotating part it has different sizes of holes from which to choose.

Shy Going, 2000; gesso, machine sewing, envelopes, copper wire, hand written; unique; 4" x 2¹/₄"

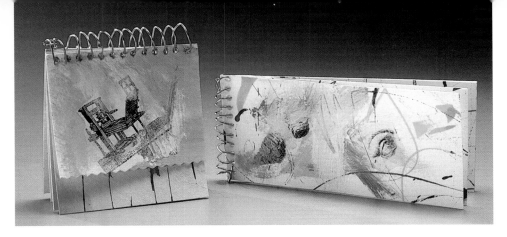

Spiral-bound wire-edge book models, 2000; blank; $3^1/2" \times 4^1/4", 2^3/4" \times 6^1/2"$

Tools: pencil, 18-gauge wire (copper or brass works well), wire cutter, rotating leather punch, $^1/2"$ dowel (approximately 8" long), binder clip or clamp to hold the pages temporarily
Materials: stack of paper (medium- to heavy-weight recommended)

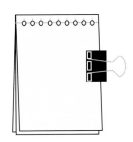

1. With your pencil, measure and mark a parallel line $^1/4"$ from the edge you want to bind.
2. Make marks at $^1/4"$ intervals along the line.

steps 1 and 2

3. Clamp three sheets together.
4. Punch holes in the pages along the line at the $^1/4"$ marks.
5. Unclamp the sheets. Place the top punched sheet on the next set of three sheets.
6. Clamp the sheets together and punch through these, using the top page as a guide.
7. Repeat steps 3-6 for the remaining sheets.

steps 3 and 4

8. Cut a length of wire that is roughly eight times the length of the spine, or edge, to be bound.
9. Bend one $^1/4"$ at one end perpendicular to the rest of the wire.
10. Take the other end and go through the far-left hole in the book (do this in reverse and go through the far-right hole if you are left-handed).
11. Pick up the dowel and hold it firmly at the edge of the book. Wind the wire around the dowel, then go into the next hole until the book is completely bound. Remove the dowel. Unclamp the book.
12. Bend the end 1/4", trim the wire if necessary, and tuck it into the spiral.

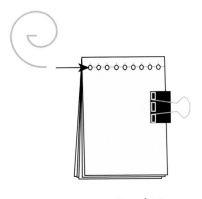
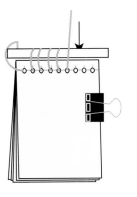

steps 9 and 10   step 11   step 12

Anne Hicks Siberell; *Paradiso XXXI*, 1999; mixed media; unique; 6" x 29" x 8" (photo by Gary Sinick)

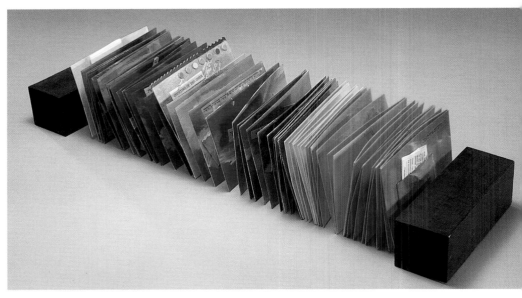

Counting the Omer, 2000; acrylics, collage, photocopies, wood; unique; 5³/₄" width x 21" depth x 3³/₄" height

CARD FILE BOOK
(SAWING, PUNCHING)

You can make tabbed cards with letters of the alphabet to create an address file or other alphabet book. To make removable cards for an interactive, change-the-story book, cut slits just under the punched holes. To make a spill-proof recipe book or book for a child, apply clear contact paper to each side of the cards.

The most involved tasks are finding the wood and dowels, cutting down the wood, and drilling four holes. Hardware stores sell the wood and dowels a bit more cheaply than art supply stores. Basswood is very soft and easy to saw and drill. You may even want to carve designs in it. One-quarter-inch dowels fit very snugly through a hole made by a standard office hole punch, which I used in this project. You might want to use a slightly smaller dowel.

I painted 51 cards for this counting book. Then I used gel medium to adhere everyday ephemera to the cards and painted on top of the collaged pieces. The dowels were painted with acrylic paint, which turned out to be a mistake, since the acrylic peels off as the cards slide back and forth over it. Instead of the acrylics on the wood, I recommend using a tiny amount of oil paint; rub it into the wooden dowels with a rag. Make sure the paint is completely dry before putting the cards on the dowels.

About *Counting the Omer*: Between the Jewish festivals of Passover (which marks the exodus from Egypt) and Shavuot (which means "weeks")

there are 49 days. It is traditional to recite a prayer, one each day, and count those days. It is said that on the fiftieth day of the exodus from Egypt the Ten Commandments would be given. The taller, removable card is the marker or bookmark that contains the prayer. The last card has a pocket that contains the Ten Commandments. Make a counting book for any holiday or birthday.

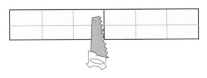

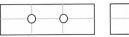

step 3

Tools: pencil, ruler, hole punch, drill or 1/4" bit and brace, saw, oil paint, sandpaper (medium)
Materials: one dowel 36" x 3/16" (or 1/4"), one block of basswood 12" x 2" x 2" (or 12" x 2" x 1"), twelve or more 3 1/2" x 5" cards, heavy paper or 2-ply board cut to size

step 4

1. Place the basswood in front of you, oriented horizontally. Measure and mark at the following places, beginning from the left edge: 2" mark, 4" mark, 6" mark, 8" mark, 10" mark.
2. Measure and draw a line one inch from the top and bottom (centered).
3. Saw the wood in half at the 6" mark.
4. Drill two 1/4" holes where the vertical and horizontal lines intersect on each piece of wood.
5. Saw the dowel in half, making two 18" pieces.
6. Sand all rough edges with medium sandpaper.
7. Rub the dowels with a small bit of oil paint on a rag. Paint the blocks of wood with acrylics or oils, leaving the inside of the holes unpainted. Let everything dry.

steps 9 and 10

For the cards:
8. Decorate your cards by painting, collaging, drawing, etc.
9. Place a card in front of you, oriented horizontally. Measure and mark 7/8" up from the bottom.
10. Measure 1 1/2" from the left and right edges. You should have 2" between the marks.
11. Punch holes in the card where the vertical and horizontal lines intersect.
12. Using this card as a template, place it over each of the remaining cards and draw inside the circles. Punch all the holes. If you are using 1/4" dowel, you may need to run the dowel through the holes to widen them slightly.
13. If you want to remove the cards or change their order once the book is assembled, cut a slit from the hole to the bottom edge. Cut a triangle, making a keyhole shape, and the cards will be even easier to remove.
14. Stack your cards in order (if you have one) and put them on the dowels, one by one, making sure that the ends of the dowels are still aligned as you go.
15. Fit the ends of the dowels into the holes that you drilled in the wood. Adjust them so they are even. If the dowels seem loose in the wood, apply glue to the inside of the drilled holes first before fitting the dowels inside.

step 11

step 13

Optional: Glue pieces of felt to the bottom of the wood to protect the display surface.

FOUND POETRY

Look in your pocket and see if you have a receipt from shopping. Does it have strange abbreviations? A poem in itself? Take a book off the shelf and read the whole words down the left hand side of the page. Does it make sense? Take out some of the words. Try again. Try another. Put in a few of your own words. I open a page of *Mary Poppins* by P.L. Travers and find: "But splashing sticking moving spaces at basket left and shouldering her talking hands."
I can rewrite it and add punctuation to get a poem:

> But splashing,
> sticking,
> moving spaces—
> a basket left,
> shouldering
> her talking hands.

That is just a first attempt. I could keep working with it. I like "her talking hands." I start adding words and revising.

> Water splashing—
> sticking to
> moving spaces in
> a basket—left
> to shower
> her talking hands.

I don't pretend this is a great poem. I could keep rewriting it to make something worth keeping. The first version was a found poem. The next is perhaps a found poem, revisited. Your choice of books will provide the tone for your poem; different authors use different kinds of words. A suspense novel will contain words that a textbook won't.

The title for *I Hide a Wild Fish Cry* came from arranging the kids' magnetic poetry that is on the refrigerator. I wanted very much to use the title for a book but didn't know how to connect this to the theme of unexpected changes. There was "fish" in the title. I tried the above technique with two books by Leo Lionni, *Fish Is Fish* and *Swimmy*: I took the first word on the left in each line. It didn't work the way I had hoped. Too many "ands." So I made a list of all the words that I liked in the two stories. From there I worked out the poems, which seemed to be nonsense. I don't know anything about fish, I thought. I went to the library and took out a few books on fishing. One was *The Essential Fly-Fisherman* and the other was *The Well-Tempered Angler*. As I learned about fly fishing I realized that my poems uncannily echoed the books I was reading. I could match up some facts about fish with a poem. Suddenly it made perfect sense. So I paired the poems with the facts; together they became the text for *I Hide a Wild Fish Cry*. (See page 112.)

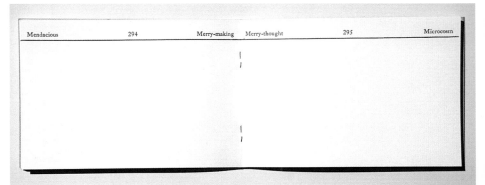

Mendacious	294	Merry-making	Merry-thought	295	Microcosm

Left: Alastair Johnston: *Cafe Charivari Charlatan Chrom*, 1975; 4^{1}/$_{2}$" x 6^{1}/$_{2}$"; linotype printed via letterpress, stapled single signature, 200 copies
Right: Alastair Johnston: *Cafe Charivari Charlatan Chrom*, open

Alastair Johnston is a letterpress printer and book artist who paired various words to make meaning in a book called *Cafe Charivari Charlatan Chrom*. The title itself is found text.

"The idea came to me one night while looking through a German-English dictionary and reading the running heads. A simple pairing like 'Pound' and 'Prattling' made me think of Ezra Pound and his declining reputation. 'Preengagement' because it is not hyphenated, made me think of 'Preen' and preening for a date. I realized other people would bring their own associations to random phrases too, so I made a quick list and set it in metal type. I don't remember why I left one page blank. The final page 'Joe' and 'Louis' was a list of boys' names, and of course Joe Louis was a famous boxer. It seemed profound at the time. Then there's all that blank space underneath that the owner of the book can use as a notebook or address book.

"Like my other concrete poetry book from the mid-Seventies, *Cafe Charivari Charlatan Chrom* was basically a one-liner that required hours of work to execute. I liked the idea of a flick-book that the reader could pick up casually and thumb through, grasp the meaning and get the joke in a few seconds (which is pretty much the attention span of most people in a bookstore)."

ALASTAIR JOHNSTON

SPELL-CHECK POEMS

"I made up a nonsense poem," shouted my then-eight-year-old daughter, Mollie, from the computer. I put down the dish, turned off the water, took off the blue rubber gloves, and went to see what she was doing. As I read the list of words I was puzzled: "flywheel"? Where did she get that? I asked her how she made the poem. She showed me.

1. Type out a random string of letters: sldfuenvbdm.
2. Break them into groupings: sld fu envb dm.
3. Hit the "spell check" on the computer. You get a list of possible words.
4. For this example, I just chose: sad fur envy do. Mollie had made a very long list, from which I liked "oh hug! edge ah juice." The spell check gives you the serendipity you may need to get fresh ideas and words you hadn't considered. A longer list yields more possibilities. For best results, avoid numbers and punctuation.

INSPIRATION FROM DAILY LIFE

In the book *The Poetry of Ikebana* by Noriko Ohno, the author mixes traditional, natural materials such as pine branches, camellias, and other flowers with found materials such as nylon netting, glass rods, and cotton for a refreshing, inspiring, and new effect. Books can also benefit from this combination of natural and unusual materials. Keep your eyes open and carry a big satchel. The unexpected treasures are waiting to be collected.

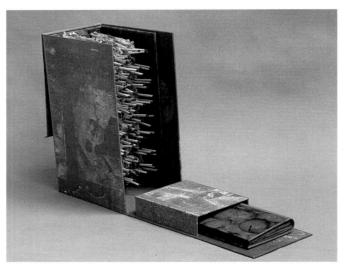

Robbin Ami Silverberg: *From Dreams to Ashes*, 1995/1999; mugwort and abaca handmade paper, wooden matches, photographic and ink-jet prints, eggshells; edition of 3; 8" x 12" x 5" (photo by R. Silverberg)

Tentative Present Memory Game (Life & Death Chess), 1999; museum board, candles, obituaries, acrylics; unique; 8" x 8" x 3"

CHAPTER 6

CLOTH BOOKS

Cloth is more durable than paper and can be used in different ways. Sewing machines become artists' tools. Canvas, embroidery mesh, and rug mesh are ideal for a textural book. Look for fabric paints, markers, crayons, rubber stamps, and pre-embroidered letters in craft, fabric, and art supply stores.

CANVAS BOOKS
(PAINTING, SEWING)

Normally, paintings are distant from us; they are on the wall and viewed from across the room. Making them into a canvas book brings them to our fingertips and allows us to change the scene if and when we like. Sas Colby, an artist who has been making different kinds of book art since the early 1970s, has made several books by painting on pieces of canvas and stitching them together.

Left: Sas Colby: *Books to Read and Write,* 1992; acrylic on canvas, applied canvas letters, French door binding; 18" x 14" (closed); unique (photo by S. Colby)
Right: Sas Colby: *Books to Read and Write*; full spread (photo by S. Colby)

Sas Colby: *Obsessive Behavior,*
1991; acrylic on canvas, mixed
media, three-panel format; 18" x 45";
unique (photo by S. Colby)

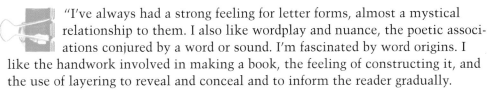

"I've always had a strong feeling for letter forms, almost a mystical relationship to them. I also like wordplay and nuance, the poetic associations conjured by a word or sound. I'm fascinated by word origins. I like the handwork involved in making a book, the feeling of constructing it, and the use of layering to reveal and conceal and to inform the reader gradually.

"I'm interested in the textural and sculptural possibilities of textiles. When I begin a canvas book I take the raw canvas, proportion the pages, and design a wraparound cover. Often, one panel of the cover is meant to be interwoven with the interior pages. Openings are usually cut to allow the reader to see through the book. I often cut the holes as the first step and then fit the text around these voids. Seeing through layers is one of the devices unique to books, and I want my books to have this complexity.

"Before deciding on the shape and size of the book, I select an appropriate canvas, which comes in various weights and finishes. Usually one side is pre-sized. I apply several coats of gesso to the raw side, then I sand it smooth. Leaving the edges raw, folding the edges over, or hemming them with heavy gel is the next decision. Heavy gel is my adhesive of choice. It dries clear and remains flexible. I attach handles with gel or stitches, which become part of the book design. For the text, I cut letters out of a contrasting weight of canvas and adhere them to the pages. I also use the gel to attach any found objects. The next step is the painting. I never sew a book together until the painting is completed. I see each painted spread as its own two-dimensional design, but it must also relate to the previous and following pages. This is the complexity of bookmaking.

"The text of *Books to Read and Write* consists entirely of categories of literature: history, fiction, romance, etc. The French door binding allows two sets of pages to interact and meet in the middle. Depending on how the pages are turned, each reading is a fresh experience. I wanted it to be like a walk through a library or a bookstore.

"In *Obsessive Behavior* my idea was to combine obsessive habits, such as counting one's footsteps, with the labor-intensive textile processes, such as stitching (one keeps at it until it is finished—total compulsion). The pages consist of grids with numbers and buttons, a pyramid built out of collected bottle caps, etc. The colors are vibrant and hyped up: it's a mad book, as in crazy. The text is a found quote about obsessive-compulsive behavior. In addition I listed my own obsessive habits. Reading it is a bit voyeuristic. I sold this book to a therapist.

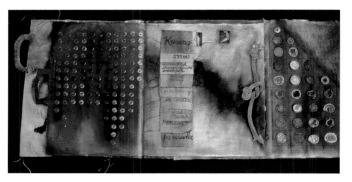

Sas Colby: *Obsessive Behavior,* open
(photo by S. Colby)

"The canvas books are really layered paintings, bringing the viewer into close contact with paint and canvas. They are meant to be seen over time: turn an occasional page and experience a different relationship of color to form to space. They are best viewed on a slanted display stand that allows the book to be fully opened on a firm support. Fragility and decay are not concerns with canvas books: they are still holding up well after ten years."

SAS COLBY

STUFFED PILLOW BOOK
(SEWING)

This book is an ideal book to give a baby or young child. Use an iron-on transfer to make a very personal cloth book, as I did in *Joseph's Family Album*, a book for my new nephew. Transfer paper is paper that is especially made to go through a copy machine. My local copy shop now advertises a "quilter's special": they will copy your image in reverse onto the transfer paper, then steam-iron the image onto a piece of cloth. This service used to be only for making T-shirts. Look for more transfer ideas in *Fabric Photos* by Marjorie Croner.

Use the same technique to make pages of a book. Trace around a cardboard template to make the cloth pages. See page 111 for details about iron-on transfers. For a finished look, use the quilter's binding on page 144.

The book will probably not stay closed if you just sew one line down the middle so you should sew two or three lines, each $1/8$" from the next.

Tools: needle, thread, sewing machine (optional, but it will save time), scissors, iron, ironing board, straight pins
Materials: six $6^{1}/2$" x 12" pieces of cotton cloth or muslin, three $6^{1}/2$" x 12" strips of quilt batting or craft and quilting fleece, thread, photo transfer paper or photo transfers

1. Use iron-on transfers, appliqué, or paint, or draw on all your pages.
2. Pair the following with their fronts together: pages 1 (cover), 12 (back cover) with pages 2, 11; pages 3, 10 with pages 4, 9; pages 5, 8 with pages 6, 7.
3. Add batting on top of one of the backs, then pin one set of pages together.

Trucks in the Sun, 2000; phototransfers, buttons, cloth, rubberstamps, beads; unique; $5^{1}/2$" x 5" x 2"

Left: *Joseph's Family Album*, 2000 cloth, color photocopy transfers; unique; 8" x 8" x $1^{1}/2$"
Right: *A Girl by Name*, 2000; laser-printed text, bridal mesh, cloth; unique; $5^{1}/2$" x $4^{1}/4$" x 2"

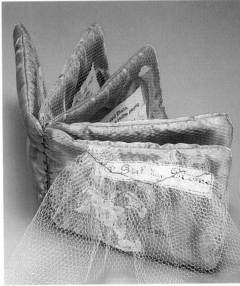

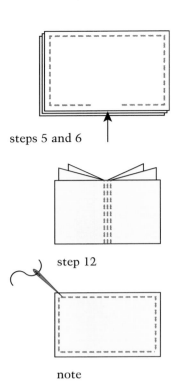

steps 5 and 6

step 12

note

4. Begin sewing in the center of the bottom edge. Sew a $1/2$" margin around the edges, leaving about 3" unsewn. Tie off all the ends of thread in square knots.

5. Unpin.

6. Turn the project inside-out. At the corners use your finger or pencil end to make the corners pointy.

7. Turn in the open edge and pin it.

8. Sew it closed with small, neat hem stitches and pull it gently but tightly. (See hem stitch on page 144.)

9. Repeat steps 3–8 for the other two sets of pages.

10. Stack the pages so that pages 2,11 and 3,10 are facing each other, and pages 4,9 and 5,8 are facing each other. Pages 6,7 should be on top and visible. With a couple of pins, pin the pages together on each side, just past the center.

11. With a pencil, lightly mark the center and $1/16$" on either side.

12. Sew a line down the middle at each of these marks. This is your spine.

13. Tie off the ends of thread and trim them.

Note: Instead of hand-sewing the hem stitch in step 8, you can use a sewing machine and sew a decorative $1/4$" quilted border all the way around the page.

RUG MESH OR NEEDLEPOINT MESH BOOK

The natural grid in the mesh can inspire all kinds of ideas. Rug mesh is very stiff and has a much larger grid. It works well for a collaged look, with bits of cloth sewn to the grid. Rug mesh is harder to find; look for it in needlecraft shops and on the Internet. It may also be called rug canvas. Needlepoint mesh has tiny holes that are spaced closer together. If you use needlepoint mesh you can use yarn to create your picture directly on the page. Or create a combination of cloth collages and needlepoint pictures on either mesh. Bridal netting forms a see-through pocketlike page that can permanently hold text and other objects. I layered the bridal mesh over the text in *A Girl by Name.*

Tools: embroidery or tapestry needle (with a large eye and blunt end), regular-size sewing needle and thread, fabric paint or acrylic paint, small brushes for paint, fabric marking pens, sewing machine (optional), scissors, pencil, ruler
Materials: Seven pieces of needlepoint (small holes) or rug mesh (wider holes) that measure 6" x 7", yarn or embroidery thread, bits of fabric, ribbons, buttons, other objects with holes (like charms, keys, beads, old coins) that can be sewn onto the cover, $1/2$" wide double-fold extra-wide bias tape (approximately 6 yards or two packages), two pieces of 12" long, 1" wide ribbon (I used wire-edged ribbon, which holds its shape)

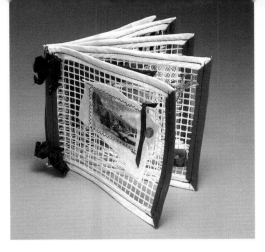

Left: *Textures of Home,* 2000; rug mesh, bias tape, photocopy transfers, etc.; unique; 7" x 6"
Right: *Catching a River,* 1993; rug mesh slipcase, letterpress printed books; edition of 40; 4" x 6³/4"

1. Cut the bias (seam-binding) tape to fit your pages; you will need two pieces that are 6" and two pieces that are 7" for each page. A little longer is better than too short.

2. Begin by sandwiching the 7" mesh page between the folds of the 7" bias tape. Align the edge of the tape with the edge of the page. Sew the tape and the mesh page together down the center of the folded tape.

3. Repeat step 2 for the opposite 7" edge.

4. Measure ¹/2" from one of the 6" pieces of bias tape. Mark it lightly on the open edge. Cut a diagonal from the folded side to the open edge.

5. Repeat step 4 for the opposite end and for the second piece of the 6" tape.

6. Sandwich the 6" side of the mesh page between the folds of one of the the 6" pieces of bias tape. Start so that the stitching from the 7" side will touch the stitching from the 6" side. Sew along the middle of the folded tape.

7. Repeat step 6 for the fourth side.

8. Repeat steps 2–7 for the rest of the pages.

9. Plan your pages so they are horizontally oriented. (The pages will turn more easily that way.) Arrange a few little collages and sew them down on the pages, one layer at a time, from the back layer to the front layer. Combine hand sewing and machine sewing, zigzag and plain for a textured look. Write text on small pieces of plain cloth or along the bias tape.

To bind the book:

10. To bind the book, take one length of ribbon approximately 12" long and poke it through the mesh from front to back (if it is easier, thread the ribbon through a large-eyed needle to do this). I started at the bottom, about two holes from the edge.

11. Pull it through so that the ends are just about even.

12. Sew to the next hole from back to front.

13. Now tie the ends in a bow or square knot.

14. Repeat for the top edge.

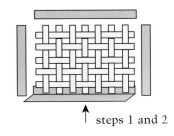

↑ steps 1 and 2

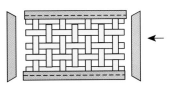

steps 4 and 5

steps 6 and 7

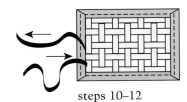

steps 10–12

CHAPTER 7

COLLABORATIONS, COMPILATIONS, AND EXCHANGES

Robbin Ami Silverberg: *Bollards*, 1998; with József Rosta and András Böröcz, photographs, rubber balls, book linen and board; edition of 5; six pieces: 16" x 6" x 6" each (photo by R. Silverberg)

While collaborations, compilations, and exchanges all involve careful planning and more than one person, each project has its own advantages and limitations. You may meet your partners or you may work independently and never meet. You may get a copy of the final book or it may be one-of-a-kind and given away. Choose a project appropriate to the particular occasion and to your temperament.

COLLABORATIONS

Two situations can provide the catalyst for a collaborative book. In one instance, you may feel confident about your writing but don't feel comfortable making images. In the other, you like your writing and your drawing, but you admire someone else's work and would like to incorporate this person's work in your book. In both cases you can make a book with the help of a partner.

Your skills may complement your partner's, but your personalities may be too different or even too similar. Be aware of the areas where you may clash. Figure out which aspects are the most important to you and discuss them. Be ready to compromise.

You may be fast at one thing and slow at another. You may be determined on some points and flexible on others. Ask yourself questions before you commit to a project. If your partner also works fast, will your piece come out sloppy? If you and your partner are both methodical, will the book ever get finished? Collaborating with someone who is very different from you can be a tremendous learning experience.

You may not always find a good collaboration partner, or you may like someone's art or writing without really knowing that person or wanting to work with him or her. If so, you may be better off either commissioning some words or images (paying for them) or asking for the work in exchange for copies of the book. This keeps the piece under your full control but doesn't allow for as rich a learning experience. Robbin Ami Silverberg is a papermaker and book artist who collaborates with many different people.

What type of collaborator are you?

fast	slow
spontaneous	methodical
confident	uncertain
determined	flexible
no limits	budget constraints
seeks challenge	realistic

"Collaboration is an important part of my work. I learned right away to be open to and respectful of another person's suggestions. In exchange for this openness and loosening of control, I gain access to another person's creative process, something I find fascinating. A true collaboration is a shared, not dictated, project.

"For *titok* ('secret' in Hungarian) I sent letters to twenty-one artists, writers, and musicians and asked them to inform or instruct me about a secret. Sometimes I altered or added to material I received or I responded to the material and created my own secrets. I then created blocks, one secret to a block, sometimes altering and destroying material I received, mixing color photocopies, transfers, black-and-white photographs, drawings, and handmade paper. The imaging on the blocks functions like a maze through which the viewer proceeds, exploring the ideas and feelings suggested about secrets. Some of the boxes are fully closed, some have peepholes, and some are open with additional boxes within. Some have hidden materials. Some smell. Some rattle. A twenty-seven–part violin piece was composed specifically for viewing *titok*. *titok* is not a linear narrative, since secrets, a priori, cannot be known or they cease to exist.

Robbin Ami Silverberg: *titok*, 1996/98; 27 4" boxes, mixed media, images made of photo, photocopy, and print; CD of violin music; collaboration with 20 artists who sent their secrets, edition of 5; 12" x 12" x 12" when closed (photo by József Rosta)

There is no one entry and no one exit. It is about reading a book by its cover, not turning the pages.

"Books are, to me, activated objects. They are culturally charged. They allow me to work with time, in rhythmic sequence. They allow for a physical relationship that is missing in almost every other art form. They can be held and touched. And books necessitate engagement also in their making: I create my own material, so content starts at the very beginning. The richest experience is when all aspects are engaged into the bookmaking: paper, binding, structure, images."

ROBBIN AMI SILVERBERG

Managing the Project

No matter how you work, if you are creating a book with a partner it may help if one of you manages the project. Managing, in this case, is not a dictatorial position, it is merely taking charge of making sure the book gets done. The book manager can say, "We agreed to have one of your drawings on this page. Can you make some rough sketches by next Tuesday?" Managing a book takes drive, organization, and the willingness to delegate some of the work without feeling that you could really get this whole thing together faster by yourself. Remember, one reason you are collaborating is that someone has a skill or style that you don't have.

General Outline for a Collaborative Book

Before you begin, decide who will finance the project and what will happen to it afterward. What is the budget? Will there be more than one copy? If not, who gets it? Will it be sold? Given away? Chopped in half with a sword? Resolving these questions ahead of time can save you major arguments and hurt feelings later. Then proceed. For help with figuring out the finances, see The Business of Collaborating, page 153.

1. Decide approximately how many copies you will make.
2. Choose the theme.
3. Decide who will write or draw or paint, etc.
4. Make rough drafts and sketches.
5. Discuss drafts and sketches.
6. Rewrite or redraw.
7. Finalize words and images.
8. Decide what materials to use (you can do this second, if you like).
9. Choose size of final project (you can do this third).
10. Figure out how much paper/material you will need.
11. Purchase or gather materials.
12. Assemble all writing, drawings, etc.

13. Cut paper or materials to size.

14. Preliminary treatment of paper/materials: paint the paper with background colors if desired.

15. Set type by hand, by computer, or write it out on the paper to cut out and paste on.

16. Print text or drawings, have them photocopied, or calligraph the text—whatever methods you chose.

17. Assemble the book.

18. Bind it and add finishing touches (ribbon, tipped-in pictures, or title strips, etc.)

COLLABORATING WITH CHILDREN

I visited an art show at the Berkeley Art Center, organized by Stanley Chan. It was about artists and their children. Some of the pieces were by the adult artists about their children, while others were collaborations between the adults and their children. Stanley Chan made collages, then asked his son to draw on top of them. While he directed what was to go where, he wanted his son to draw in his natural style. I liked the collaborations very much.

I took my then-seven-and-a-half-year-old daughter to the exhibit and asked her what she liked the best. She didn't like the collages as much as I did. She liked the pieces of slate on which children had drawn with oil pastels, and she liked a mobile that had pictures on one side balanced by a mesh bag of words on the other. I asked her if we collaborated how she would want to work with me. She asked if our piece would go in the gallery.

When I asked her again, she seemed bored and pulled out a book of reproductions of paintings by well-known artists. We had looked through this book before, and I asked which paintings she liked and why. Sometimes she liked the subject matter, sometimes the colors. She seemed most interested when I asked whether if I wrote poems she would like to illustrate them. I have seen many books about bookmaking that have great ideas for books to make with children, but for my daughter they are not satisfactory. She is interested in making something that an adult might make. She can sense if it is intended for children and tends to reject it if it is.

When you work with your own child, the children in your classroom, a grandchild, niece, nephew, or friend, let them know that what they are doing is important to you. In *Literacy Through the Book Arts*, Paul Johnson demonstrates wonderful ways of using books in classroom collaborations; all the children work on a story together then brainstorm ways to present it. Individuals make their own books using the class story.

A few months later I noticed a refrigerator-magnet poem that my daughter had written. I liked it very much and asked if I could make a book out of it. At first she got very excited. I said I would like us to paint the paper together and then I would print on top of it; she agreed. We got out the acrylic

A Pink Magic Bubble, by Mollie Budiansky, 1999; letterpress-printed text over acrylic inks and gesso-stenciled rectangles; edition of 35; 2³/4" x 3" x ³/8" (photo by Jim Hair)

inks. When she saw how many sheets of paper I wanted us to "decorate" (15 pieces), she got tired. I had to cajole her into finishing the last five pieces. She began to paint big, thickly inked words that I knew wouldn't dry or look very good when we cut the paper to size. I ran over and scribbled on top of the words with a dry brush, exasperated. She thought this was funny and did more of these words on other pages. I ran over with my dry brush to "save" the paper. It became a game. We worked fast. I turned the papers around to get the top of the sheets. And then I saw that these papers would be the best of the lot. They were spontaneous, uncalculated, and really fun. I had tried to over-manage my daughter and she rebelled.

I cut the paper into strips, then stenciled some rectangles on each page, evoking the refrigerator magnets. I printed handset type on top of the rectangles. The final result was the book *A Pink Magic Bubble.* We gave a copy to each of her elementary school teachers on the last day of school. They were pleased. Mollie was proud.

What a Child Might Like to Do

Depending on the age, a child might be interested in:

1. Lettering the title page or specific words in the text.
2. Drawing a cover illustration or making images for the whole book.
3. Writing his or her own poem or short story.
4. Drawing on stencil paper, eraser, or linoleum block that an adult then carves and prints or that the child rubber-stamps.
5. Looking at postcard reproductions and then either painting in another artist's style or using the same colors for an original painting that can be used as the cover or frontispiece, or that can be reproduced.

Circle Accordion Book
(FOLDING, TAPING)

This is my favorite structure because it is so simple.

Tools: scissors or knife and cutting mat, self-adhesive linen tape, bone folder, pencil, metal-edged ruler

Materials: five pieces of medium to heavy paper, 6" x 22" long, grained short. These can be cut from a 22" x 30" sheet of printmaking or drawing paper

1. Pick one piece of paper to be your cover. Cut off $1/2$" to make it 6" x $21 1/2$". Measure $10 1/2$" from each edge, and mark and score. You should have a $1/2$" spine in the center.

2. Fold each edge in to the closest center fold. You may want to score the paper first at the $5 1/4$" mark.

3. With the remaining sheets, cut 1" off the edges to create four sheets that are each 6" x 21".

4. Fold one sheet in half widthwise, right-side in. Crease it well with a bone folder.

5. Keeping the paper folded, bring one end back to the middle fold.

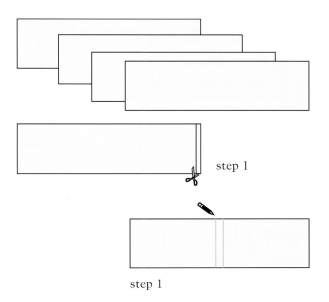

step 1

step 1

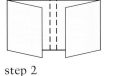

step 2

step 3

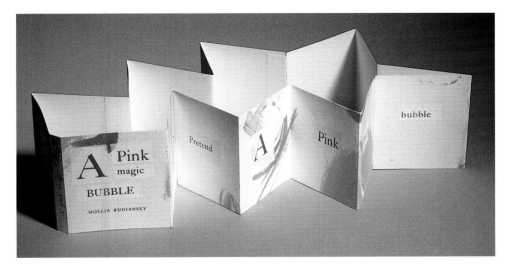

A Pink Magic Bubble by Mollie Budiansky, 1999, completely open (photo by Jim Hair)

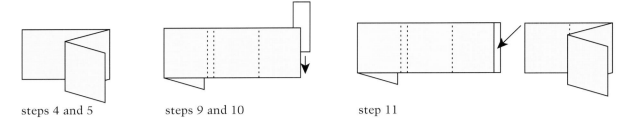

steps 4 and 5   steps 9 and 10   step 11

6. Turn the paper over and bring the other end to the middle fold.

7. Repeat steps 5 and 6 on all four sheets.

8. Cut five 6" lengths of linen tape.

9. Start connecting the pages by placing the cover piece in front of you, face up.

10. Take the backing off one piece of the tape. Attach the tape to the edge of the cover lengthwise, sticky-side up, leaving half the sticky side available.

11. Attach the next page by aligning it with the cover end and pressing down on the available half of the tape.

12. Continue to tape and attach pages until you get to the last one. Tape the last page to the back flap of the cover in the same manner.

COMPILATIONS

In academic circles there is the custom of the *Festschrift,* which is German for "festival writings." When a scholar is to be honored, such as for a birthday or celebration of many years of teaching, colleagues and admirers write academic articles and essays. These writings are collected and a publisher is found. The publisher may be a scholarly journal or an established commercial publisher.

A tribute or birthday book has the flavor of the *Festschrift,* except that the writings and images are personal and *you* are the publisher. You may assemble photographs, jokes, anecdotes, a time line or biography, songs, photocopies of favorite objects, collages that depict the honoree's interests, or anything else that will lie flat in a book.

Tribute or Birthday Book
(SEWING)

For my mother's birthday we sent out instructions to thirty people, along with a sheet of archival paper. Each person decorated the page and sent it back in the large, self-addressed envelope that we included. I assembled the pages and bound them into a handmade book. Use a sidebound structure such as the one described under *Exquisite Corpse Book,* on page 94, but do not cut the pages into thirds.

Alphabet Star Book
(FOLDING, GLUING)

Three Dimensions in the Alphabet,
2000; laser printed, model;
$4^1/4$" x $5^1/2$"

A friend organized a gift book for me when I was expecting my first child. She assigned each of my friends a letter of the alphabet and told them to make a page with that letter. After they sent back their pages, she slipped the illustrated alphabet into plastic sleeves in a commercially made notebook. For a handmade book you could make a larger version of the *Pocket Frame Book,* page 52, or the *Alphabet Star Book.*

For *Three Dimensions in the Alphabet* the images were taken from Dover pictures on the CD *MasterClips,* which contains thousands of clip art pictures. The typeface is Americana Bold. The structure is a marriage of a Japanese album-style book and a star book. While this one is only a model, I could have planned an edition of the *Alphabet Star Book* because it could be easily reproduced.

If you decide to organize a compilation, you can either assign the letters and give the paper to the participants or give the participants the specifications.

Tools: pencil, scissors or art knife and cutting mat, PVA or glue stick, scrap paper
Materials: twenty-six sheets of $8^1/2$" x $5^1/2$" paper, grained short, twenty-six strips of 2" x 7" lightweight paper, grained short

1. Draw, collage, or write on the large sheet of paper about things that relate to the letter.
2. Fold the paper strip in half widthwise. Open.
3. Draw the letter, centered, on the strip, making the letter 2" tall.
4. Measure $1/2$" from top and bottom of the strip. With a pencil, lightly draw two lines at these places that are parallel to the longest edges of the paper.
5. Cut out the edges of the letter above the top line and below the bottom line, leaving the letter connected to the paper in the middle. Also make a cut along the top line and the bottom line, again, leaving the letter connected to the 7" piece of paper.

steps 2–5

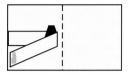

step 7

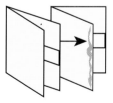

step 8 and 9

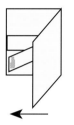

step 10

steps 12 and 14

6. Fold the large sheet of paper in half widthwise. Open.

7. Put a thin line of glue on the back of the left side of the letter strip.

8. Press down, aligned with left edge of the larger paper. Fold the letter strip over so it is "closed."

9. Put a line of glue on the back of the right side of the letter strip.

10. Close the larger paper on top of the strip and press down.

To connect all the completed sheets:

11. Put a sheet of scrap paper inside the very last page. Face it so that it is open (fore edge) to the right, the folded edge on the left.

12. Spread the glue in a thin, flat line along the fore edge.

13. Remove the scrap paper and discard it, replacing it with a sheet of waxed paper.

14. Set the next-to-last page on top. Line it up and press it down.

15. Continue steps 11–14 from back to front until all the pages are glued together.

16. Press under weights overnight.

A variation of this book may be made with sewn layers of accordion-folded pages (see the photo of Julie Chen's book *Radio Silence*, in Accordion-Fold Books, page 31.)

Compilation Suggestions

If you do decide to try one of these projects, consider several things.

1. If you send people the paper that is to be included in the book, send it with a stiff backing and a self-addressed envelope. Remember that people are busy; make it as easy as possible for them to complete and return the pages.

2. If archival quality is important to you, choose the paper yourself and send it to the participants. Non-archival paper can become brittle, yellow, or spotted over time.

3. Keep your instructions simple. Even the most well-intentioned people may not remember them. If the instructions are too complicated, they won't be followed.

4. Be clear in explaining that you have a specific idea in mind. Tell people that everyone needs to follow the guidelines for the project to work.

5. Always include a phone number, email, and address in your packet and encourage questions. For a compilation or exchange to work, make it easy for participants to ask questions so they won't have to guess.

Editions

The convenience of computer-generated and photocopied books is that the edition can be unlimited. Using a computer to set type also allows the book artist to create a longer book with more text. This would be time-consuming if one had to set many pages of type by hand and print it with a letterpress. Photocopying is relatively inexpensive, and if you decide you'd like to sell your work, you can charge a reasonable price.

Traditionally, editions are signed and numbered. The numbering system can look like a fraction: 1/50, which means copy number one of a total of fifty copies. Or you can write it out in words. Copy number one doesn't necessarily mean it is the best of the edition or the first to be made. It is merely an identifying mark.

EXCHANGES

While it is fun to create a one-of-a-kind book, you can also create an edition of a book that incorporates pages from different people.

In 1991, I sent requests to twenty-five letterpress printers to make a page for an exchange book. I gave the dimensions and told them to leave a one-inch margin on the left-hand edge of a horizontal page. I received pages from fourteen people. Two people did not leave a margin. Remember to give specific instructions, but try to plan your book so that the limiting factors are few; even the most well-intentioned people do not read carefully. Each person printed fifty copies of their page. I collated the pages and bound fifty small books. Each participant received three copies of the book.

Although I liked the bound-book format, the contributing letterpress printers and rubber-stamp artists were interested in making postcards instead. They felt they could use the extra cards they printed, but not the extra pages of a book. So I switched formats and made a small box to contain the cards. The themes were broad, and, I hoped, provocative in some way. I expressed my desire for the contributors to merge words and images in one piece.

Catherine Michaelis organized an exchange for a printer's deck of cards based on a project of large-scale, quilted cloth cards. She called the project *Stack the Deck* and asked the participants to work with the theme "women's health and healing." Twenty-two letterpress printers participated; each was assigned three cards (jokers, title, and index cards were included). (See pages 8, 103, and 122.)

Letterpress printing is not required for this type of project. A group of women poets in the San Francisco Bay area create an ongoing poetry journal called *Rooms*. Each participant sends fifty photocopies of her piece plus a nominal postage fee. The organizers collate and bind the poems and send a copy of the collection to each contributor.

Top: *Print Exchange Book*, 1991; edition of 50; 6" x 4"
Bottom: *Print Exchanges*, 1992–1995; varying editions of 50–75; 6" x 4"

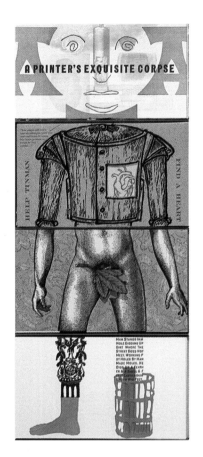

Exquisite Corpse Book

One of the Surrealist games of the 1920s, *Cadavre exquis* got its name from the first sentence that appeared the first time the game was played: "The exquisite / corpse / will drink / the new / wine."

The Silver Buckle Press at Memorial Library at the University of Wisconsin at Madison organized *A Printer's Exquisite Corpse.* Each printer was assigned a segment of the body: head, upper torso, lower torso, and feet. The size of the card was specified, with marks on the card determining where the participant's segment should go. The final cards were printed in an edition of 100, collated and placed in a beautiful handmade box that had dividers in it so that one corpse could be displayed at a time. The project was so successful that a few years later the press launched a second project called *Exquisite Horse.*

One particularly exciting exquisite corpse book is *Emandulo Re-Creation.* Robbin Ami Silverberg organized the project at Artist Proof Studio, a printmaking facility set up for black artists in South Africa. Nineteen South African artists, one artist from Ghana, Robbin, and her husband András (both professional artists themselves) each made a full-size print depicting a creation myth. The prints were then cut in half and each half cut into thirds to create two exquisite corpses, which were bound into an accordion-style spine.

Left: Silver Buckle Press: *A Printer's Exquisite Corpse,* 18¹/2" x 21¹/2"; cards from top to bottom by: Silver Buckle Press; Bonnie O'Connell, The Penumbra Press; M. J. Pauly, Lychnobite Press; Alisa Golden, never mind the press
Right: Robbin Ami Silverberg: *Emandulo Re-Creation,* Artist Proof Studio and Dobbin Books, 1997; edition of 30; 17¹/2" x 12" x 1" (photo by József Rosta)

Exquisite Corpse Model, 2000; collage and acrylics on paper; unique; 6" x 9"

This exchange proved dynamic as Robbin did not tell the artists where the body parts were to end exactly; only which quadrants to use. Sometimes the legs are in the middle, sometimes on the side, sometimes there are no legs.

This use of the exquisite corpse format is also conceptually interesting as it literally created a mix between a wide range of artists of both different artistic styles and also cultural and racial backgrounds.

Create your own exquisite corpse and put it in a book with pockets. Or make a flag book, adhere it to an accordion, color-photocopy the pieces, and make a folded pamphlet or other accordion or ox-plow book. The following are instructions for making a sidebound, softcover, exquisite corpse book. The proportions of your exquisite corpses will not match actual living humans.

Tools: binder clip, awl, cardboard to protect table, needle, thread, metal ruler
Materials: six sheets of 6" x 9" medium-weight paper, grained short; two 6" x 9" sheets of heavier cover paper
Example: 6" x 9"

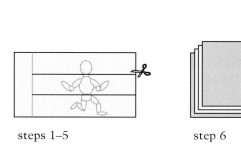

steps 1–5

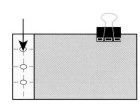

step 6

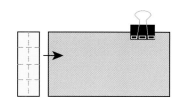

steps 7 and 8

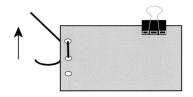

step 9

steps 10 and 11

1. Measure and mark the pages so that they have a border of one inch on the left side.
2. Measure the pages so that they are divided into thirds. Draw light pencil lines to help you.
3. Draw a figure with the head in the top third, the neck just ending at the middle third. Make the torso and arms in the middle third. Use the bottom third for the legs and feet.
4. Create different figures for each page or ask other people to make their own page.
5. Using an art knife against a metal ruler, cut a slit from the right edges to the one-inch border.
6. Assemble the pages in a neat stack. Put covers on the front and back.
7. Use a jig or ruler to measure for three holes. For a jig, use a strip of paper the same height as the book and one inch wide. The holes should be $1/2$" from the left edge.
8. Clamp the whole stack with a binder clip.
9. Poke three holes with the awl, making sure you have cardboard underneath to protect your table.
10. Use a length of thread approximately three times the width (head to tail) of your book. Do not knot it. Leaving four inches of thread, start sewing from the middle hole, from back to front.

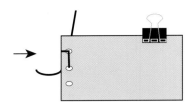

steps 13 and 14

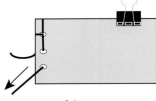

step 14

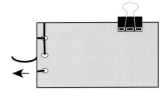

step 15

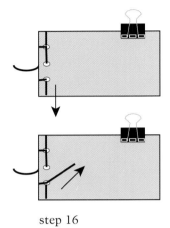

step 16

11. Take the thread to the top hole from front to back.

12. Take the thread around the left edge of the book (from back to front) and go back in the top hole.

13. Now take the thread from the top hole over the head of the book (from back to front) and back into the top hole again.

14. Skip the middle hole and sew into the bottom hole from back to front.

15. Take the thread around the left edge of the book (from back to front) and go back in the bottom hole.

16. Take the thread around the bottom edge of the book (from back to front) and go back in the bottom hole.

17. Sew into the middle hole (back to front)

18. Take the thread around the side of the book and back into the middle hole. You should now have two tails of thread on the back.

19. Put one tail of thread on each side of the long stitch. Tighten all stitches. Tie the two ends of thread together into a square knot.

20. Trim the ends to $1/8$" to $1/4$" from the knot.

step 17

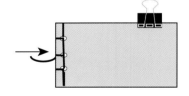

step 18

step 20 (complete)

Organizing an Exchange Project

1. People don't like to read instructions, but to make a successful project, you will need to set guidelines and pass out information. Be very clear and simple.

2. You will need to charge a small fee for postage unless you are financing the project yourself.

3. Limit your number unless you have volunteers to help collate. I suggest that 50 cards are manageable, 30–40 preferable.

4. If you are making a wrapper or box, limit the size you will accept and be ruthless: send back the cards that are too big. Or make a wrapper or box that can accommodate different-size cards. Make it easy on yourself.

5. Send back cards that are stuck together or that have offset onto the back of the next card. Chances are, they are going to stick to or rub off on someone else's card as well.

6. Encourage people to send a self-addressed, stamped postcard if they want acknowledgment that you have received their cards. This reduces the long-distance phone calls.

7. Keep a sheet of paper near the envelopes. Write down the name, address, and phone number, whether the participant has paid, and any other information you may need. It's easier to do this one at a time as the envelopes arrive than when you have fifty of them. Use the information on this sheet to type up a list of names to give to each participant and/or make mailing labels.

8. If you have a theme or flier for the next year, save mailing costs and send it with this year's cards.

9. Choose a name that best reflects the kinds of card you would like to receive.

10. Continue the project as long as it is fun.

Rotating Notebooks

In this exchange each artist begins with a blank book of her own choosing. She may make one by hand or purchase one at a stationery or art supply store. Each artist draws or writes on one page, then passes it on to the next person in the group until everyone has created a page. You will then have as many unique books as you have participants. This is not an edition but a kind of series. I recommend giving each participant a time limit so that the books are finished in your own lifetime. Give each artist a month to do a page. Find a place like a public library to exhibit all the books or have a book party if the participants all live near one another. The following are instructions for a multiple-signature, softcover book that works well for this project.

Tools: art knife, cutting mat, linen thread, awl, pencil, ruler, needle, self-adhesive linen tape the height of the finished book (in this example that would be 7")

Materials: two pieces of cardlike paper (such as printmaking paper) 22" x 30", grained long

Rotating Notebooks, 2000; 6" x 7¹/₂"; by Patricia Behning, Alisa Golden, Lynne Knight, Marc Pandone, Val Simonetti, Nan Wishner, Yoko Yoshikawa

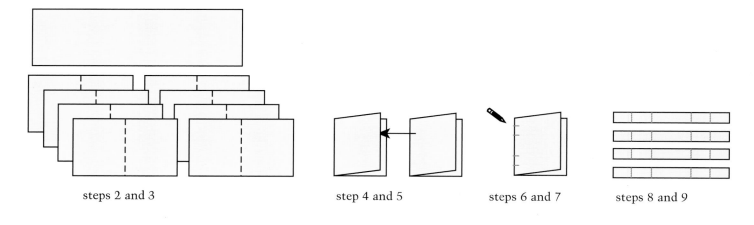

steps 2 and 3   step 4 and 5   steps 6 and 7   steps 8 and 9

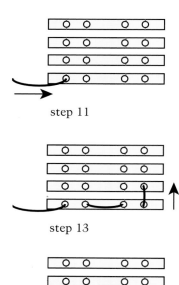

step 11

step 13

step 14

step 15

step 16

1. Cut the paper into strips that are 6" x 22" (paper will now be grained short).

2. Set aside one piece of 6" x 22" for the cover.

3. Cut four pieces in half so you have eight pieces of 6" x 11".

4. Fold each of those eight pieces in half.

5. Nest them in pairs. You will now have four signatures with two pieces in each signature.

6. Measure and mark 1" from the head and tail of one of the signatures.

7. Also measure 2" from the head and tail and mark it. Use this signature as a guide to make similar marks on the other three signatures.

8. Keeping the signatures folded, rest each of the signatures on top of one another and align the spines. The marks should be aligned as well. Face the spines toward you.

9. Make a notch with your knife through all the signatures at the marks, or poke holes with your needle.

10. Thread a needle with about 20" of thread. Do not knot it.

11. Leaving 3" of thread, sew from the outside of one of the signatures to the inside, starting at the head.

12. Sew a running stitch to the tail of the book (in and out; you'll end out).

13. Sew from the outside of the first signature to the outside of the second signature.

14. Sew a running stitch now to the head of the book.

15. Tie the ends of the thread in a square knot. Do not cut the thread.

16. Add the third signature and sew from the outside of the second signature to the outside of the third signature.

17. Sew a running stitch to the tail of the book.

18. Do a kettle stitch here to connect the third signature to the second and first signatures. (See page 142 for the kettle stitch.)

19. Add the fourth signature and sew from the outside of the third signature to the outside of the fourth signature.

20. Do a running stitch to the head of the book.

21. Do a last kettle stitch.

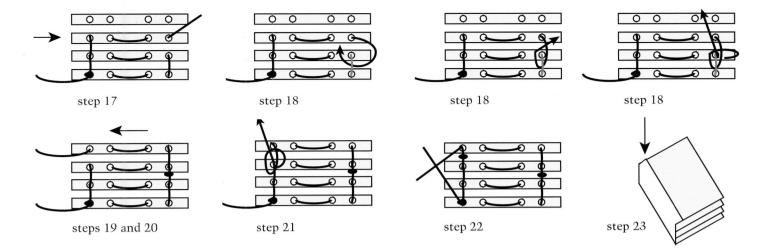

step 17

step 18

step 18

step 18

steps 19 and 20

step 21

step 22

step 23

22. Tie the ends of thread together one last time and trim them.

23. Apply the self-adhesive linen tape across the spine of the book, tightly covering the stitching.

Rotating Notebooks, open; back row: *Le Royaume du Ciel,* by Patricia Behning, page by Patricia Behning; *Loose Edges,* by Lynne Knight, orange page by Yoko Yoshikawa, green page by Alisa Golden; *Logdark,* by Nan Wishner, page by Nan Wishner; front row: *Guide from Thin Air,* by Marc Pandone, page by Val Simonetti; *The Hope That Is Under My Skin,* by Alisa Golden, page by Lynne Knight; *i scream u scream,* by Val Simonetti, page by Marc Pandone

Folding the cover:

24. Measure and mark the center of the piece of 6" x 22" strip. Do not fold it.

25. Make a mark 1/4" from either side of the center mark. These will be your fold marks. You are creating a spine that is 1/2".

26. Erase the midline mark.

27. Indent one of the other marks with your thumbnail; fold the paper so that the indent is exactly where the fold is (You may choose to make a score line first). Align one edge of the paper with itself as you fold it over.

28. Repeat step 27 for the other mark.

29. Measure 5⁵/₈" out toward the edges from each of these new folds. Make marks there.

30. Indent or score, then fold at the marks.

31. Turn the paper over. Write your title on the spine, if you like. Decorate the cover paper with rubber stamps or acrylic inks (optional).

32. For an optional front window, put your cover right-side up in front of you. Cut out a rectangle in the panel that is third from the left (second from the right). Don't count the spine area as a panel.

33. Wrap one flap around the first page of the book, one page around the back of the book.

34. Using the piece you cut out of the window as a guide or as a backing paper, make a small collage or drawing and adhere it to the front page of the book, so that it is just showing inside the window.

35. Glue down the front flap to the first page so that the small collage will stay aligned in the window.

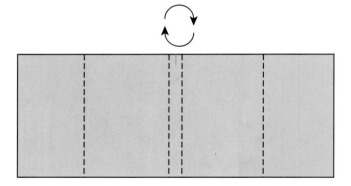

steps 24–31

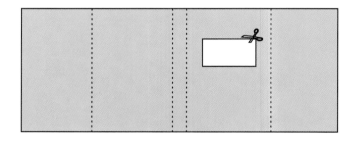

step 32

CHAPTER 8

LAYERS AND RECESSES

U se layers and recesses to give your book depth and meaning on different levels. One layer can contrast dynamically with another for a more playful and meaningful presentation. Add physical texture and visual shadows to your book by creating recesses that can highlight small objects.

LAYERS

One example of layers appears in the work of the Japanese artist Hon'ami Koetsu, who worked in the 1600s. He wrote on top of scrolls painted by other artists. Sometimes the poems he calligraphed seemed to have no connection to the paintings beneath them. Each of his pieces takes on new meaning as the viewer strives to understand the relationship of the words to the image. Even though the layers seem very different, the viewer still tries to connect them.

A very old, layered book was rediscovered in 1998: a tenth-century manuscript called the *Archimedes Palimpsest*. Archimedes' text about mathematical physics was scraped off the parchment, leaving very faint writing. Then the text of a twelfth-century prayer book was written over and perpendicular to Archimedes' original text. I am intrigued by layers of writing, especially when one text runs vertically and the other horizontally, as in the *Archimedes Palimpsest*.

Palimpsest (Greek for "rubbed again") used to refer only to parchment or vellum. I first heard the word in reference to twentieth-century poetry by H.D. (Hilda Doolittle). You can make a book with a palimpsest theme: a life

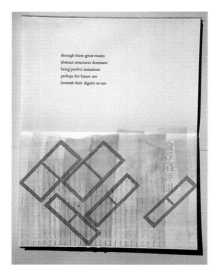

Top: Alastair Johnston: "become a major barrier," from *Muted Hawks,* by Tom Raworth, 1995; 6¹/2" x 9³/4"; handset type, letterpress printed, "hot printing," accordion-fold book; edition of 40 (photo by A. Johnston)
Bottom: Alastair Johnston: "through these great rooms abstract structures dominate" from *Muted Hawks,* by Tom Raworth, 1995; 6¹/2" x 9³/4"; handset type, letterpress printed, "hot printing," accordion-fold book; edition of 40 (photo by A. Johnston)

that changes, one story with different endings, how a house or an object or article of clothing gets passed from one owner to the next; palimpsest can refer to anything that has semi-visible layers of history. Layers can be visual, such as the words erased and redrawn, or physical objects such as torn papers. Alastair Johnston used both kinds of layers when he created the book *Muted Hawks* by Tom Raworth.

 "Hearing Tom Raworth read at New College of California, San Francisco, inspired me to do the book *Muted Hawks.* His poems are short lightning bursts aimed at the political establishment and public complacency. When he reads, you feel as though you are hearing many voices; I thought of the layered walls of a metropolis rendered illegible by nervous idlers ripping at the marketing posters that adorn our streets.

"I also thought of Dutch revolutionary printer Nicolaas Werkman, who, when his business was a failure, closed the doors and began to make art out of the materials in his shop. The press was too constricting so he put type on the floor, inked it up and rubbed paper over it like Japanese woodblock printers. Freed from the constraints of the press and the tyranny of 'type height' he found that many objects, such as door plates, brass handles, wood, bits of fencing, etc., could be inked up and an impression taken. He then began applying ink directly to the paper with a brayer, and cut shapes out of tympan material for a stencil. Werkman called this 'Hot Printing'—like Hot Jazz, which was all the rage in the 1930s when he was working. He was shot by the Nazis on the last day of the war in Holland.

"Using material in my print shop: furniture, wood type, found process zincs, etc., I tried recreating some of Werkman's techniques for this book. I had no preconception about any of the images and added layers till they were done, or in some cases, overdone. The forty copies are more or less identical. There are twelve poems and twelve prints: they get denser as the book progresses. One page 'open to exploitation by experts' was inspired by frescoes at Pompeii (in terms of shape and color) because I had been there the previous summer. On the pages with bits of words, I thought about the gaudy woodtype posters in the Third World that I had photographed on other trips. After I inked the type, I laid torn paper over it to create a mask. I used lots of masking tape for an irregular base to many of the prints. Occasionally I included blind-embossing, which I highlighted with a brayer.

"The finished pages were tipped together into a long accordion. The slipcase has a linoleum block, printed in pale gray, over silver of the title.

"My favorite page is one of the simplest, titled 'abstract structures dominate.' For this one I laid down a mottled background directly with an inked brayer. Then I tore open a light-bulb carton and mounted it so I could print the corrugations in gray blue. Over that I printed some large metal furniture in turquoise and five words in a purplish tint in Chinese. I have no idea what they say. Maybe there's further profundity in there!"

ALASTAIR JOHNSTON

Health & Healing Cards for *Stack the Deck*, 1999; letterpress printing; 5" x 7¼" (photo by Jim Hair)

For my *Health and Healing Cards*, part of Catherine Michaelis's project, I used a letterpress to print many layers for each print. First I used acrylic gel medium to adhere string and other objects to a piece of wood. After I applied three coats of gel and let them dry, I inked up the block and printed it with black ink. Over this I printed a faint gray linoleum block. Then I carved the linoleum block further, rotated it, and printed it again with a darker gray. I repeated the process with an even darker gray. On top of these four layers I printed other images and handset type.

PAINTED PAPER

Mix gesso with acrylic paint to prepare paper for a book. The result is a colorful, toothy surface that readily accepts pencil and ink. The addition of the gesso makes the acrylics less sticky and shiny (so the pages won't stick together). Gesso comes in white, black, Venetian red, and sometimes a yellow-gold.

Painted Ox-Plow Book model, 2001; acrylic inks, gesso, rubber stamp; 3" x 3"

Left: Anne Hayden Schwartzburg: *Point Reyes Fire,* 1996; 19" x 24", open; mixed media on paper; unique (photo by m.y. ono)
Right: Anne Hayden Schwartzburg: *Sogno: Italia,* 1997; 22" x 29", open; gouache and ink on paper; unique (photo by m.y. ono)

Anne Hayden Schwartzburg: *Sogno: Italia,* detail of different page (photo by m.y. ono)

You must use a medium- to heavy-weight paper for these techniques. Painting both sides eliminates the curling that occurs when only one side is painted. You can paint each side a different color. To prevent sagging and buckling paper, don't add any water to the paint.

Look for a printmaking paper or a good drawing paper with a high cotton or rag content with a weight of 250 g/sq. meter or more. Begin to work with a large-size paper and cut it down with an art knife or paper cutter. It is much less intimidating working big and knowing you will be cutting it up. You can't make a mistake.

Acrylic Inks

I have tried different water media and like acrylic inks best. Make sure the inks are labeled "acrylic inks" and not calligraphic inks or watercolor inks. I recently used some other ink and was startled that the finished product smelled of ammonia. Acrylic inks are generally lightfast (check this, too), which means they won't fade over time, and they are permanent, which means that if they get wet again they won't run. Use the inks full strength: the colors are brighter. Adding water to them will likely make your paper sag and buckle. I try to use lighter or brighter colors because when I try to draw or print atop the painted paper, even black ink won't show on top of dark blues and purples. Use different widths or kinds of brushes, dip pens, sticks, or other utensils you can dip into the ink. If brushes intimidate you, pick up sticks from the sidewalk and use those; they make interesting marks.

Anne Hayden Stevens (née Schwartzburg) uses a variety of media, including images she has first drawn on the computer. She is the one who first inspired me to layer the pages with paint when we collaborated on a book, *Tidal Poems.*

"These books are about remembering something carefully. I generally start in book form with a series of folded, unbound sheets of paper. I first touch the pages all over with paint or ink. Then I gradually layer in drawings and pace the handwritten text through the book, working with either liquid inks or gouache. I turn my memories over and over in the making process: re-sequencing images of places or people, cultivating a textual voice with a pitch and timbre that fits the drawings, and working the texture of the page's surface. I am trying to recreate my experiences for others in a way that provides the reader a mood and pace close to what I feel.

"The wildfires in the Point Reyes National Seashore in 1996 were the first natural devastation of a land I knew well. I remember standing in front of my office in Berkeley and watching the ash drift down at me, large white flakes of burnt matter, and feeling that my landscape was being irrevocably changed and there was nothing I could do. I was moved to make the book by a trip to Limantour Beach after the fire, walking up the green watersheds and seeing burnt trees ankle deep in water. The land was not devastated; it was oddly beautiful and powerful.

"I woke up one morning after a vivid dream, reached for a notepad and wrote down the text of *Sogno: Italia*. I was half awake, and when I returned to the text I was surprised to find that it was a complete narrative, with a pace and timbre that captured the mood of the dream. I made the book to see if I could ground such a wandering story in imagery, and see it spread and unfold with some kind of coherence. It was this book that began to lead me into painting, as tensions between the diverse page spreads made me begin to consider the strength of the images on their own, without text.

"I worked my way into my thesis by writing with gesso on a white sheet of paper which became this book, using the north light coming through the studio windows in Wurster Hall to articulate the letterforms with the briefest shadow. In this study book I sorted out the themes of my written thesis, writing and layering the ideas freely before beginning to sort them into more linear form. This gentle way of working helped me unfold my thesis ideas in my own language before constraining them with more thesis-like form.

"The best part about making books is watching readers interact with them. Watching their eyes and hands move across a work reveals the book's true successes and weaknesses. The body doesn't lie, so the artwork can be evaluated wordlessly, and as the maker I can silently follow the reader through the story, over and over again."

ANNE HAYDEN STEVENS

Anne Hayden Schwartzburg: *Thesis Book*, 1997; ink, pencil, and wax on paper, folded book from one sheet of paper; unique; open: 18" x 24", closed: 9" x 6"
(photo by Craig Sherburne)

Materials: acrylic inks (no black, dark blue or dark purple), a variety of sizes and shapes and widths of brushes, dip pens, feathers, sticks, straws, other drawing implements, large stencil brush to use dry.

1. Think about the feeling of your book. Does it correspond to a season? Is it about earth or water or fire? Is it about childhood memories? Pick three or more inks that evoke this feeling and that look good together. I like to pick

colors that harmonize, such as varieties of blue/purple/silver or green/brown/gold, so I can keep working and not worry if my colors are going to get muddy. Blue with orange, red with green, and yellow with purple should be allowed to dry before using their complementary mates, or you will behold much brown.

2. On your large paper begin by writing one word or sentence over and over.
3. With a dry brush scribble out any wet ink. You can move your hand in circles or use a back-and-forth motion.
4. Take your next color and make a big shape or several shapes.
5. With your third color, fill in some of the places where shapes intersect as if you were coloring them in.
6. Use a thinner brush and write more words or make lines.
7. Rinse out your brushes immediately or keep a jar of water nearby to put them into until you can rinse them.

For a textural effect: Pour a thin layer of ink into a plastic lid or small shallow dish. Crumple up a paper towel or clean cloth. Dip the towel lightly in the ink, then blot it all over the paper you want to decorate. Let dry before you continue with a second color. Some manufacturers of acrylic inks make shiny or "pearlescent" colors. Most make an almost-metallic gold and silver (the silver usually looks more like gray, however).

Gessoed Stencils

I stenciled white rectangles over painted paper in Mollie's book *A Pink Magic Bubble*. On top of the rectangles I printed words. The white rectangles made the words easier to read. (See pages 88–89.)

Materials: art knife and spare blades, cutting mat or cardboard to protect your work surface, pencil, one sheet of Duralene (a type of drafting vellum), white gesso, flat-bottomed stencil brush

1. Draw a square or rectangular window on the Duralene.
2. With your art knife, cut out the window.
3. Place the stencil over your project, where you want the window to appear.
4. Dip your stencil brush into the gesso, just lightly wetting the ends of the brush. Apply the gesso through the stencil by tapping with the stencil brush. The taps are perpendicular with your work surface. For crisp edges, don't make strokes: the gesso may leak under the stencil.

PASTE PAPERS

Paste papers are made from a paste and paint mixture and traditionally are used as endpapers in a book. They also make good-looking covers, wrapping paper, and accents. You can make the process as complicated or as simple as you like. You are working with a mixture of wheat paste or methyl cellulose

Next Door, 2000; paste paper, laser-printed text; unique; 5³/4" x 3³/4"

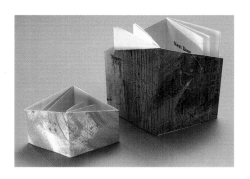

and acrylic paint and some texturing tools. Some people use old credit cards cut with different-shaped notches or texturing tools found in the hardware store.

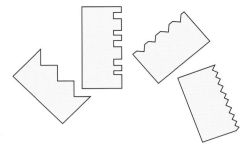

Texturing tools

The first time I attempted paste papers I was overwhelmed by the color and texture choices. I couldn't get the lines perfect without overlapping them. So I settled for random lines and hand prints. Complementary colors like yellow/purple, red/green, and blue/orange will make brown if they are mixed. Experiment with different kinds of color and texture to find ones you like.

When you are finished, you can use the painted paper as a treated surface on which to add text or images. I like the look of a colorful background with a strong black image on top. If your lettering is too spindly or light, it will look confusing. Don't make the reader have to work too hard to read the words; it is frustrating and many readers will give up.

If you are working with children, they may be disappointed when they find out you are going to cut the paper into pieces or fold it up. A pattern of lines or designs, cut or folded up, is less likely to bother them than their picture of specific images. Paste papers, painted on both sides, make interesting origami papers as well.

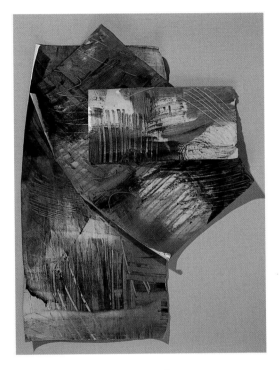

Paste Paper Samples

Tools: different size brushes, wheat paste, acrylic paints, empty pint containers (like yogurt or cottage cheese), bits of cardboard or old credit cards, toothpicks, other objects
Materials: medium-weight paper

1. If you are using powdered wheat paste, prepare a batch of paste by adding powder to cold water, a little at a time, until you have a thick, stiff consistency that can stand up on its own.
2. Divide the wheat paste into containers.
3. Squeeze about an inch of the acrylic out of the tube into each of the containers. Use one container for each color you desire.
4. With a large brush, spread the paint/paste mixture thinly and evenly until the surface of the paper is covered. Pick off the lumps of wheat paste. You can use different colors like a patchwork or random design.
5. Draw designs in the still-wet paint/paste with a credit card cut into a sawtooth, or with toothpicks or other objects.
6. Let dry.
7. Add different colors on top, if desired, and draw again.

PENCIL OR CHARCOAL

I learned the following technique from Marc Pandone, an artist and art teacher in Northern California. To prepare the paper, begin by using charcoal (pencils or sticks) or a soft, dark drawing pencil. Keep a rag, chamois cloth, or dry paper towel nearby. Also have a white plastic eraser or an Artgum eraser on hand. If you are using the dark pencil, have some white gesso nearby as well. If you are using the charcoal you will need an acrylic spray fixative. Use this spray outdoors on a non-windy day. It's unhealthy to inhale this spray, which has an unpleasant odor.

A charcoal drawing will have deeper tones and a gray background. A pencil drawing can be enhanced by taking small amounts of gesso and rubbing them into the paper across the pencil marks. Scrub it in as if you were trying to remove a spot. You can even paint over the whole page; gesso won't cover the marks completely with one coat. I like to use the wooden end of a brush to scribble in the wet gesso as well. The gesso leaves a nice toothy surface on which you can continue to draw with plain or colored pencils. Watercolor pencils are good for this. After you draw with the watercolor pencils, you can dip a small brush in water and paint over the pencil with the water.

1. Place a large piece of medium-heavy printmaking or drawing paper on your work table.
2. Think about a scene or memory. Focus on an object that was present at that time or visualize the landscape. Begin to draw the shapes. Don't worry if it is accurate.
3. After five minutes, wipe the paper with the cloth (if using charcoal) or erase the marks (if using a drawing pencil).
4. Redraw the same image in a different spot or draw a completely different scene.
5. Rub out the marks again.
6. Write something about this memory across the rubbed-out drawing until you fill the paper.
7. Rub out the writing.
8. Continue drawing, rubbing out, writing and rubbing out the marks until you have built up an interesting-looking surface. The point is to prepare your paper, not draw a perfect picture.

TYPEFACES

Words add another layer to a drawing or painting. Large-size words can be used as single images, rows and rows of tiny text can look like a pattern or lines. Use words and text together to create a mood or story.

You may choose a certain typeface or write the words by hand, depending both on the kind of book you are making and your access to other equipment.

William Blake used his skill as an engraver and familiarity with printmaking to make his own books as early as the late 1700s. He wrote text by hand directly on metal plates, which were then inked and printed.

Henri Matisse worked on painted paper cut-out illustrations for his book *Jazz* in the 1940s. He wrote the text himself "because he couldn't think of an appropriate text that already existed." He decided to use his own handwriting after seeing Picasso write out some poetry by hand and liking how expressive it looked. *Jazz* was published in an edition of 250 numbered copies. Matisse's handwriting added to the visual imagery of *Jazz*. Use your handwriting for a personal and intimate feeling.

Where do you start if you want to use type for text? According to *The Chicago Manual of Style* your eye can comfortably read 65–70 characters of type per line. The number may vary, depending on the size and kind of the type. Twelve-point type is standard for the text of books, 14 point for children's books. But your book may be large and need 18 or 24 point text on its oversized pages.

You may want to mix typefaces. A face with serifs is most easily read for the body of the text. Use a bolder face without serifs for titling. Use fancy display, if you like, for the title of the book. I like to pick three faces that are completely and obviously different. Don't use typefaces that look too much alike.

Underneath a painting may lie a story. Hide text that is too personal by first writing it on paper or printing it out, then painting over part or all of it. Write text on top and paint over it again. Then write the story you want to reveal on the very top layer. Create your own palimpsest.

COMPUTER-BASED DRAWINGS

Using the computer as a tool is an excellent way to make layers. Because of the computer's unique capacity for memory it is possible to save a drawing at any stage, redraw, or go back to the part you liked. Variations on a theme are endless. Anne Hayden Stevens takes her computer-based drawings one step further.

Anne Hayden Stevens: *Kosovo Diary*, 1999; inkjet, gouache, and ink on paper; sidebound with sewing machine stitching, gatefold in the centerfold; unique; 6" x 9" (photo by Craig Sherburne)

"I'm drawing on the computer in essentially the same way that I draw on paper; I work with a pressure-sensitive tablet and stylus and a program called *Painter*. Every time I make a new stroke or add color, make a line or add shading, the program records it as a separate step. I can replay the stages of the drawing at any time.

"In the case of *Kosovo Diary*, I played back the first 20 strokes to create the initial framework of the drawing. Then, in a new image, I played back the first 60-odd strokes to see the framework and more details such as the buildings and figures. I used this technique to create six different drawings from two original images. After importing the drawings into Quark Xpress to lay out the page structure of the book, I printed out the spreads with an ink-jet printer. To complete the drawings, I painted with watercolor, pencil, and gouache on top of the ink-jet prints. I bound the book using a sewing machine and archival adhesive.

"Painting in the computer allows me to explore the drawing process in a way that I cannot do when I work physically with paints and inks. At the same time, the printing process lacks the tactile quality of the written or painted surface. My current explorations look at ways to integrate digital drawing's capacity for repeated steps with the intimacy of the handwritten mark."

ANNE HAYDEN STEVENS

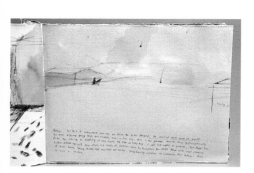

Anne Hayden Stevens; *Kosovo Diary*, 1999; inkjet, gouache, and ink on paper; unique; 6" x 9" (photo by Craig Sherburne)

TRANSFERS

Use a transfer technique when you want to use a photograph in your book. Waxed paper transfers produce somewhat cloudy, pastel-toned images. Iron-on transfers made from color photocopies and specially made transfer paper yield crisp, bright pictures. Chemical transfers produce an image that is somewhat in-between.

Waxed Paper Transfers

With this transfer technique you can take an object from one picture and place it in another. The picture will be slightly faint. If it is too ghostly, your newspaper may be too old and the ink all dried up.

Tools: waxed paper, bone folder
Materials: newspapers, paper onto which you want the transfer, such as printmaking or drawing paper

1. Place waxed paper on top of the picture you want to transfer.
2. Rub the waxed paper vigorously with the bone folder until you have covered the entire image.

3. Pick up the waxed paper and place it on the drawing paper where you want it to be.

4. Rub the waxed paper vigorously again, the same way you did in step 2.

5. Take away the waxed paper. The image should be there.

Iron-On Transfers

If you want to work with photographs or printed text, you can photocopy onto a special transfer paper that runs through some photocopy machines and some laser printers. Some copy shops can do this for you.

To transfer the images:

1. Set your iron on the highest heat.

2. Put the cloth faceup. Protect all cloth that will not be imprinted by putting clean paper over it.

3. Put the transfer facedown.

4. Hold the iron down on the back of the transfer paper for 10 seconds, then quickly peel it off. You must peel it straight and not diagonally or the image will be distorted.

For more transfer techniques, see *Fabric Photos,* by Marjorie Croner.

Chemical Transfers

Another transfer effect can be achieved by using a colorless blender, which is an inkless marking pen sold with a large assortment of design markers. The colorless blender contains a solvent that will transfer photocopies from their original paper to a second sheet. The drawbacks are that the photo will be in

Picnic Recipes, 2000; waxed paper transfers, removable cloth cover, handwritten recipes, plastic ants, plastic tablecloth; unique; 7" x 11"

reverse and the solvent is toxic. Use the pen outside or in a well-ventilated area.

1. Place the paper you desire in front of you, faceup.
2. Place the photocopy wrong-side down where you want it to go.
3. Uncap the colorless blender and rub it all over the back of the photocopy.
4. Remove the photocopy and discard it.
5. Don't inhale.

RECESSES

Recesses add three-dimensional, physical depth to artwork. You can make a recess in a book cover in one of two ways. The first way involves using two or more 2-ply boards that you glue together. The second way involves partially cutting into a 4-ply board and peeling off a layer or two. In a recess you can place a title strip or a thin object. I used a recess to give shadow to the cover of *Distressed* and to protect the reader's fingers from a tied fly for the book *I Hide a Wild Fish Cry*.

Large or Deep Recess

1. Cut two covers exactly the same size from a 2-ply board.
2. Decide where you want the recess and measure and mark a window on one cover board only. Cut out the window.

I Hide a Wild Fish Cry, 1999; acrylics, letterpress, linen thread, tied fly; edition of 10; 3³/4" x 7³/4" (photo by Jim Hair)

3. Apply glue to the back of the board with the window. It will probably be less awkward if you leave the window board faceup and press the unglued board on top of it instead of trying to move the glued window board. Align the edges of the two boards and press them together.

4. Put the laminated boards between two sheets of waxed paper and leave them under a heavy weight overnight. Use a 4-ply board for the back cover.

Note: If you want a thicker cover with a deeper recess, cut more boards with windows and glue them all together.

For a mysterious effect:
1. Cut out two extra pieces of two 2-ply board and cut the windows in these, also.
2. Glue a layer of drafting vellum or glassine between the two extra sets, making the "glass" for the window of your recess.
3. Glue this "sandwich" on top of the window of the previously made set.

Note: If you want your front and back covers to feel evenly weighted, make a plain back cover of 8-ply board (any combination of boards glued together, as necessary).

Small or Shallow Recess

The second technique involves no glue. I recommend it for small recesses under a couple of inches in width and length.
1. Take a piece of 4-ply board and measure and mark a recess.
2. With your art knife next to a metal ruler, cut into the board about halfway.
3. Use the knife to loosen the edges.
4. With your fingers or a tweezers, pull up the layers of board to make a uniformly flat recess. If you are having trouble pulling up the layers, you may have either not cut deeply enough into the board or you have made your recess much too large.

DISTRESSED BOOK COVERS

A student showed me some polymer clay book covers she had made in a class. She had made marks and dents in the clay, then rubbed it with paint. I liked the concept but I didn't like the final texture. The baked polymer clay felt funny and not very durable. I tried a similar technique with layers of museum board and was very happy with the results. I used them for the cover of my one-of-a-kind book *Distressed*. It is a long poem about stress and trying to get things done too fast. Adding layers and recesses to the covers gives the book a pleasing physical texture.

Left: *Distressed,* 1998; acrylics, distressed cover, letterpress, iron-on transfers; 4¹/2" x 5³/4"
(photo by Jim Hair)
Right: *Distressed,* 1998
(photo by Jim Hair)

Tools: 4-ply museum board, PVA or gel medium, acrylic paint, stencil brush, hammer or mallet, art knife and spare blades, self-healing cutting mat, sandpaper
Objects with which to make marks: paper clips, hardware such as screws, bolts, picture hangers, nuts, keys, old metal type, needles or pushpins to poke holes, cookie cutters, other metal objects that have distinctive shape or texture
Materials: boards for covers, random strips of 2-ply or 4-ply boards

1. Make dents and marks in the board by hammering objects into it, then removing the objects. Scratch the board with keys, paper clips, or needles. Poke holes with pushpins. Enjoy doing a little damage. With your art knife, cut a sawtooth pattern into one of the edges, or just cut some slits.
2. Glue down strips of 2-ply or 4-ply board that have either been cut or torn or both. Cut a window in one or two of the strips to make a recess, if you like.
3. Take a very tiny amount of two different colors of acrylic paint, enough to wet the brush, and scrub the paint into the board, one section at a time. Add more paint and continue until the board is covered.
4. Paint the back of the board, too, so it doesn't warp. (You don't need to paint the back of the board if you will be applying glue to it later, such as for a cover of an accordion-fold book.)

CHAPTER 9

CONTAINERS: PROTECTION AND DISPLAY

You can wrap books. You can encase them in plastic. You can also make a holder, such as a display stand for a hanging book. You can display a sculptural book by using wood, found materials, or even paper mâché. Julie Chen carefully chooses materials for her boxes that reflect and enhance the meaning of her book's text.

Julie Chen: *Bon Bon Mots*, 1998; letterpress printed from photopolymer plates on a variety of papers; edition of 100 copies. Box size: 10" x 7" x 1³/₄"

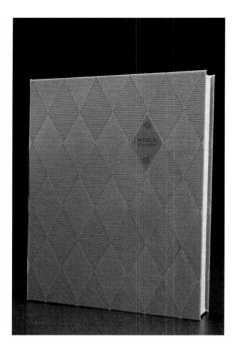
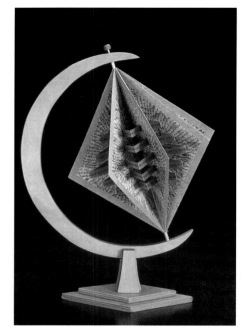

Left: *World Without End,* 1999; box:
12" x 15" x 2"
Middle: *World Without End,* 1999;
letterpress printed from photopolymer plates on a variety of paper
including found maps; edition of 25;
book: 4¹/4" x 10" closed, book on
wooden stand: 11" x 15" x 8³/4"
Right: *World Without End,* 1999; in
box with inserts

"During the past twelve years of making books, the box has become increasingly important to my work. More than just an elegant and prac-tical form of storage, the container is an integral part of the reading experience. The box is the first step in creating an atmosphere that helps to pre-pare and focus the reader on the book itself.

"While all my books include some kind of box or portfolio covering, some-times the box itself is a key element in the piece. This is especially apparent in *Bon Bon Mots,* a boxed set of five small books that I designed to resemble a box of exquisite confections. Each book presents a text that is complete in itself. The box, with its satin lining and gold title sheet, defines the overall meaning of the piece, drawing the five individual books into a unified whole.

"A large clamshell box contains the book and a wooden stand for the book *World Without End.* Its size, color, and diamond-patterned fabric are meant to remind the viewer of a large, old-fashioned atlas that might have been encoun-tered during childhood. This initial impression prepares the reader: when they open the box, they find a set of objects that, when fitted together, allow the reader to display the book like an unusual globe, complete with map imagery and a wooden globe stand.

"I have always been fascinated by the sculptural potential of the artist book form, both the structure of the book as well as the packaging. I find that the box contributes to the 'objectness' of the piece: the book can be viewed as an artifact as well as simply a book."

JULIE CHEN

REMOVABLE CLOTH COVER
(SEWING)

Year after year a woman called me saying she was interested in making books but she wanted them to be practical. She said she was thinking of something like a cloth book cover.

Tools: sewing machine or needle and thread, pins, pencil, ruler, iron and ironing board or pad of scrap cloth or Pellon (interfacing), scissors, scratch paper on which to take notes
Materials: cloth

1. Open the book you want to cover.
2. Measure the length of the book (the width of each cover plus the depth of the spine and the spaces between the spine and the covers). Write this down.
3. Measure the height of the book (from head to tail). Write this down.
4. Add 8" to the length.
5. Add 2" to the height.
6. Cut your cloth to the size you noted in steps 4 (length) and 5 (height).
7. Iron a $1/2$" hem all the way around. Mark and pin first if necessary.
8. Open the cloth back up. Cut a small triangle off each corner. See diagram.
9. Fold the sides back to how they were ironed down.
10. Sew hems at the right and left sides.
11. Fold the cloth around your book to make equal-size pockets at the right and left sides. Remove the book carefully. Pin the cloth into place.
12. Sew a hem across the top and bottom.
13. Tie off the ends.
14. Tuck the book in the front and back pockets.

Picnic Recipes, 2000; 7" x 11".
Remarkable Women, 2000; muslin with iron-on transfers; $1^{1}/_{2}$" x $5^{3}/_{4}$"

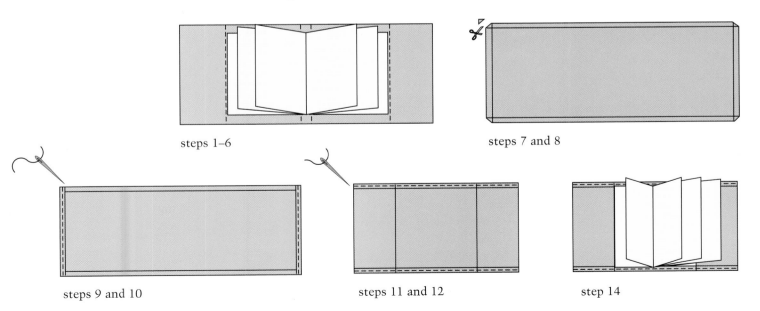

steps 1–6

steps 7 and 8

steps 9 and 10

steps 11 and 12

step 14

Left: *Traveling Sketch Book Model,*
2000; double-sided paper;
$4^3/4$" x $5^3/4$" x $1^1/4$"
Right: *Traveling Sketch Book Model,*
open

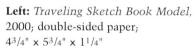

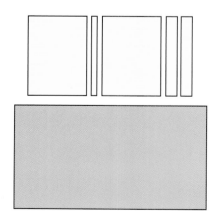

steps 2 and 3

TRAVELING SKETCH BOOK
(GLUING)

The holder will accommodate a vertically oriented journal or sketch book in the right pocket with a left pocket for postcards, tickets, etc. You will need a book that is bound at the top, or you can make your own. (See page 120.)

Tools: ruler, scissors, PVA or paste/glue, $3/16$" metal spacing bar, bone folder, pencil, old magazines for scrap paper, glue brush, art knife, and cutting mat
Materials: two 4-ply boards $4^1/2$" x $5^3/4$", two 4-ply boards 1" x $5^3/4$", one 4-ply board $7/8$" x $5^3/4$", one cover paper $12^3/4$" x $7^3/4$", one piece of sturdy, soft (easily folded), medium-weight paper for the pocket 4" x $10^1/4$", one endsheet $5^1/2$" x $12^1/2$", 30" of ribbon
  1. Cover your work surface with the scrap paper.
  2. Arrange the pieces of board from left to right as follows: $4^1/2$" x $5^3/4$", $7/8$" x $5^3/4$", $4^1/2$" x $5^3/4$", 1" x $5^3/4$", 1" x $5^3/4$".
  3. Place the cover sheet in front of you, horizontally oriented, wrong-side up.
  4. Leave a 1" margin from the left edge.

Begin applying PVA/paste in sections:
  5. Apply enough glue to adhere the left board. Press the board into place.
  6. Apply glue to adhere the $7/8$" strip of board. Abut the spacing bar to the right edge of the board. Press the strip of board into place. Remove the spacing bar.

7. Continue to work, alternately applying glue, then pressing a piece of board into place. Use the spacing bar when positioning each board.

8. Cut diagonals at the corners of the cover paper, leaving a slight margin between the cut and the board.

9. Apply glue to each edge flap, one at a time, turning these edges in and smoothing them down.

10. Apply glue to the back of the endsheet. Press into place.

Add the pocket:

11. Of the paper that will be the pocket, measure and fold $1/4$" on the short edges, right and left.

12. Fold the pocket paper in half lengthwise, with the folded edges in. Open.

13. Apply a thin line of glue to one half of each of the folded edges. Press together to make the pocket.

14. Apply glue to the back of the pocket. Press down, aligned with the left edge of the covered boards, on top of the endsheet.

15. Press between waxed paper under a heavy book overnight.

Attach the ribbon:

16. Measure halfway between head and tail. Make marks in the gap between the $7/8$" strip and the second $4^1/2$" x $3/4$" board from the left, in the gap after this board, and two places just inside the next 1" strip. Use your art knife and cut slits here that are the same width as the ribbon.

17. Starting from the left-hand side, thread the ribbon from the outside to the inside, across the second board, then make a little loop for a pencil on the 1" strip. Come out the back.

18. Slip the back cardboard of the sketch book under the ribbon and into the pocket. Tie the covers closed.

Note: It may help to push the ribbon through the slits with a butter knife, palette knife, or other thin, flat tool.

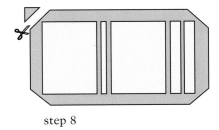

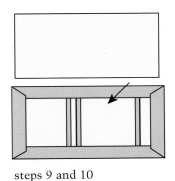

step 8

steps 9 and 10

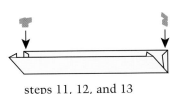

steps 11, 12, and 13

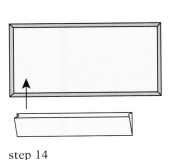

step 14

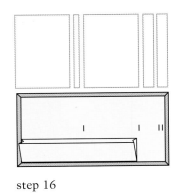

step 16

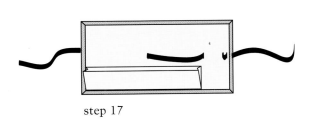

step 17

Sketch Book
(GLUING)

Make a sketch book or notepad of any size with this method. Expose the shorter side if you are making the traveling sketch book holder. If you put something other than a regular pencil in the holder, make the sketch book 1/4" narrower. Allow enough room so that the cover will close properly.

Tools: PVA glue or padding compound (found in some stationery stores), heavy book, glue brush or piece of board with which to spread the glue
Materials: A 3/4" to 1" stack of 4 1/4" x 5 1/2" paper, 4 1/4" x 5 1/2" piece of cardboard or 4-ply museum board

  1. Align the stack of paper on top of the board so that a side is hanging off the edge of the table by about an inch. Expose the shorter side if you are making the sketch book holder above.
  2. Put the heavy book on top of the stack.
  3. Spread glue thickly on the exposed edge. Let dry.

Note: For a journal you will need a front cover board also. Use only the PVA. When the book is dry, add a strip of self-adhesive linen tape, or glue a strip of decorative paper over the bound edge, wrapping the strip around the front and back covers.

MATCHBOX-STYLE BOX
(GLUING)

If you want a longer-lasting box, use cotton rag paper. For a larger box, like the one that contains *Oh, Great Chicken,* use paper that is a little larger than the size of your book plus a margin on all sides of twice the depth. The box for the above book measures 3 1/2" x 8" x 1"; the paper used was 7 1/2" x 12".

Tools: pencil, ruler, art knife, cutting mat, bone folder, PVA
Materials: cereal box or stiff paper (250 gm/sq meter printmaking paper or card stock) 3 1/2" x 2 1/8"

For the bottom of the box:
  1. Arrange paper vertically. Measure 3/8" from top and bottom edges. Mark and score lines horizontally.
  2. Measure 3/8" from those top and bottom scores. Mark and score these second sets of horizontal lines.
  3. Measure 3/8" from right and left edges. Mark and score lines vertically.

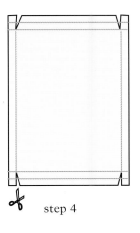
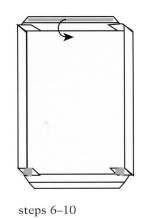

step 4   steps 6–10

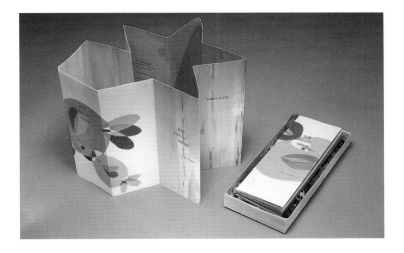

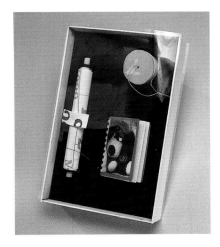

4. Make slits along the vertical lines just up to the second horizontal scores, top and bottom. You need to cut just a sliver out of the top and bottom mid-sections (see diagram).

5. Fold all scores.

6. Bend and fold the flaps up toward you.

7. Fold the right and left sides so they are perpendicular to the rest of the paper. You are making box sides.

8. Take a small bit of PVA and put it on the back of the flaps.

9. Fold the top edge up and press to the flaps.

10. Run a thin line of glue across the top edge and glue to what will be the inside of your box.

11. Repeat steps 8–10 to make the fourth wall of the box.

Variation: Make a 5" x 8" x 1$^1/_2$" box out of heavy paper that measures 9$^1/_2$" x 11". For steps 1–3 measure 1$^1/_2$" instead of $^3/_8$".

For the top of the tiny box: use paper 4$^1/_8$" x 3$^1/_8$." For a display box, or box with a see-through top, use a piece of Mylar cut to 4$^1/_8$" x 3$^1/_8$." If you choose Mylar, you will need to use a bone folder to make very tight creases.

1. Turn paper horizontally.

2. Mark and score (from left to right) four vertical lines to make five sections with the following widths: $^3/_8$", 1$^3/_8$", $^1/_2$", 1$^3/_8$", $^1/_2$".

3. Fold all scores.

4. Put a thin line of glue on the right flap.

5. Wrap the right flap around to meet the left flap.

6. Glue what will be the inside of the right flap to the outside of the left flap. Hold in place until the glue has set. If you are using PVA, this should be about a minute. If you use Mylar, you may want to connect the lid flaps with self-adhesive linen tape.

Note: To customize your tape, paint the tape with acrylic paints and gesso first before you adhere it.

Top: *Oh, Great Chicken,* 2000; letterpress printed text, handpainted paper, Mylar; edition of 15; 3$^1/_2$" x 8" x 1"; circle accordion book 2$^3/_4$" x 7$^1/_4$"

Bottom: *Memory Box,* 2000; insert with three books: scroll, circle book, soft-cover multi-signature book; unique; 5" x 8" x 1$^1/_2$"

step 2

Catherine Michaelis: *Stack the Deck*, 1999; 5" x 7¹/4"; exchange project

HARDCOVER-BOX BOTTOM
(GLUING)

For a sturdier bottom to your box, build it out of 4-ply museum board (¹/16" thick). Cut a piece of board for the base that is ¹/2" wider and ¹/2" taller than the item you intend to display.

Example: You have a book that is 4¹/2" x 7¹/2". Its box should be 5" x 8".
Materials: Use one board for the base that is 5" x 8", two strips of board for the walls that are 1¹/2" x 8", two strips of board for the shorter walls that are 1¹/2" x 4⁷/8" (this allows for the thickness of the longer walls when you glue the box together), PVA, four squares of self-adhesive hinging tape to reinforce the corners.

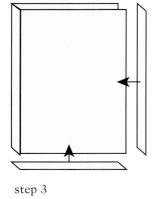

step 3

1. Apply glue to the edge of one of the 1¹/2" x 8" strips. Press it down on the 5" x 8" baseboard, aligned with the edge. Hold for 30 seconds or until set.
2. Apply glue to the edge of one of the 1¹/2" x 4⁷/8" strips; also put glue on one of the ends. Press this one onto the 5" x 8" base and abut to the 1¹/2" x 8" strip that is already in place.
3. Continue building the box until all four sides are secured to the base, and to each other at the corners. Put a square of linen tape on the inside of each corner for reinforcement.

For a Mylar lid for the above example:
4. Put a piece of 8" x 14" Mylar in front of you horizontally.
5. Measure and score ¹/2" from the left edge.
6. From the score, measure and score 1⁵/8".

7. From the second score, measure and score $5^1/8"$.
8. From the third score, measure and score $1^5/8"$ again.
9. From the fourth score, measure and score $5^1/8"$.
10. Wrap the Mylar around the box.
11. Center a 9" strip of self-adhesive linen tape across the loose ends of the Mylar.
12. Take the Mylar off of the box.
13. Wrap the leftover $1/2"$ of each end of the linen tape around the edge of the Mylar and press it down on the inside.

DISPLAY STAND FOR A HANGING BOOK
(SAWING, DRILLING)

This size stand works for a vertically oriented book 4" x 5", bound on the 4" side.

Tools: pencil, bit brace and $1/4"$ bit, handsaw, hammer, a few 1" brads or awl/ice pick/pointy object to make a thin hole, small piece of medium sandpaper, PVA

Materials: $1/4"$ dowel, 2" x 7" x 1" piece of wood, 18-gauge wire

1. Saw the dowel into two $6^1/2"$ pieces and one 7" piece.
2. Sand the rough edges of the dowels (and sand off any stickiness from price tags or labels if applicable).

Shrine to the Shadows, 2000; acrylics, wood, dowels, copper wire, waxed-paper transfers; unique; 7" x 7" x $1^1/2"$; book 4" x $5^1/4"$

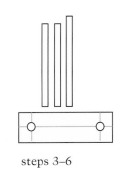

steps 3–6

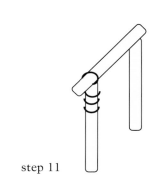

step 9   step 10

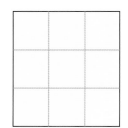

step 11

3. With your pencil, measure and mark 1" from the right and left ends of the block of wood.

4. Draw two lines at these marks that are parallel to the ends.

5. Measure 1" from the top edge of the wood and make marks on each of the parallel lines.

6. With the bit brace and the $1/4$" bit, drill a hole at these two intersecting marks.

7. Fit the $6^1/2$" dowels snugly into the holes. You may glue the dowels into the holes with PVA for added security.

8. With the pointy object make tiny holes in the center of the top of each dowel. (If you use a brad, pull it out again.)

9. Cut 3" of wire and coil it completely around one of the $6^1/2$" dowels. Leave it coiled around the dowel.

10. Pull up the top end of the now-coiled wire and poke it into the tiny hole in the top of the dowel. Make sure this end forms a loop.

11. Shape the loop so that the 7" dowel will fit through it and rest on top of the $6^1/2$" dowels.

12. Put a drop of PVA into the hole and poke the wire back into it.

13. Repeat steps 9–12 for the other $6^1/2$" dowel.

14. Slide the 7" dowel into the two loops. This dowel will always be removable so that you can take a book on or off the display.

15. Paint the display with acrylic paints if you desire.

THEATER BOX: A Tunnel Book
(CUTTING, GLUING)

Make a three-dimensional book in a box that works like scenery in a theater. The pieces are removable and interchangeable so you can make as many scenes as you like.

Tools: art knife, cutting mat, ruler, PVA glue, scissors, pencil, bone folder, self-adhesive linen hinging tape
Materials: 2-ply board $12^1/2$" x $14^1/4$" (for the box), $5^1/2$" x $7^1/2$" (for the lid), 12 strips of 4-ply board $4^1/4$" x $1/2$"; **cover paper:** $5^1/2$" x 22" (for the box), 6" x $3^3/4$" (for the bottom of the box), $6^1/2$" x $8^1/2$" (for the lid); **Mylar:** $5^3/4$" x 4" (for the front of the box), $6^1/4$" x $4^1/4$" (for the lid), six pieces of $4^1/2$" x $6^1/4$" 2-ply board (for the scenes)

Building the box:
1. Place the $12^1/2$" x $14^1/4$" board in front of you vertically.
2. Measure and mark $4^1/4$" from the right and left edges.
3. Measure and mark 4" from the top and bottom edges.
4. With your art knife against a ruler, make light scores connecting the top and bottom marks and the right and left marks, making what looks like a tic-tac-toe grid.

steps 1–4

BreakfastScape, 2000; acrylics, museum board, Mylar; unique; $6^1/2'' \times 4^1/2'' \times 4^1/4''$

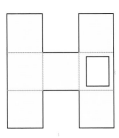

steps 5–8

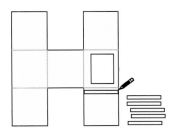

steps 9 and 10

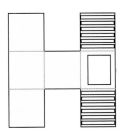

steps 10–14

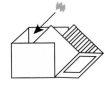

steps 15–17

5. With your art knife against the ruler, cut out the top and bottom middle sections. Your board should now look like a capital "H".

6. In the right-hand middle section you will be outlining and cutting a rectangular window. Measure and mark $1/2''$ from the right edge and $1/2''$ from the top and bottom of this particular section.

7. Measure and mark $3/4''$ from the left side of this section.

8. With your art knife against the ruler, cut out the rectangular window.

9. Now you will glue down the strips of board. Start measuring and gluing from the side below and closest to the cut-out section. Progress toward the outside edge. Mark $1/8''$ from the top edge of the middle section.

10. Glue down one strip of board so that one edge touches the $1/8''$ mark.

11. Measure another $1/8''$ from the edge of that board.

12. Glue down another strip of board.

13. Continuing measuring and gluing until you have $1/8''$ space, $1/2''$ board, space, board, space, board, space, board, space, board, space, board.

14. Repeat steps 9-13 for the top edge of the cut-out section.

15. Fold up the box along the score lines with the paneled sections visible on the inside.

16. With the linen hinging tape, tape the unpaneled sides to the bottom of the box.

17. Apply glue to the flat side of the paneled flaps and press them to the standing walls. Hold them together for about a minute or until the PVA is set.

Covering the box:

18. Now you will cover the box. Start at the back of the box (the side without the window). Glue your $5^1/2'' \times 22''$ piece of cover paper so that approximately $1^1/2''$ cover the back of the box. Leave a top and bottom margin of about $3/4''$ (at least $1/2''$).

19. Apply glue to the next side of the box and rub down the cover paper.

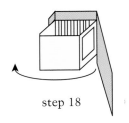

step 18

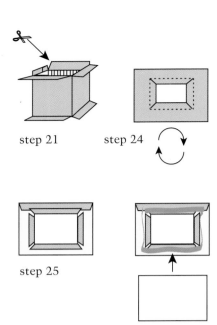

step 21   step 24

step 25

step 26

20. Continue to apply glue and press down the paper until all four sides are covered. (You will cover up the window.)
21. Cut very thin triangles or slits at each of the eight corners.
22. Apply glue to each flap of cover paper and rub down one by one.
23. Apply glue to the 6" x 3³/4" paper and cover the bottom of the box.
24. Make diagonal slits from each of the corners where the window will be. Trim down the points of these triangular flaps to about ¹/2" from each edge of the window.
25. Apply glue to each flap and cover the edges of the window.
26. Run a line of glue around the border of the window on the inside of the box. Press the 5³/4" x 4" Mylar into place. Hold for about a minute.

Building the lid:
27. Measure and mark ¹/2" from each edge of the 5¹/2" x 7¹/2" piece of board.
28. Lightly score this tic-tac-toe grid with your art knife.
29. Cut slits from the edges in, parallel to the long sides only.
30. Cut a shape in the large middle panel. You may also cut a rectangle that has at least ¹/2" margin all the way around. This will be your top window.
31. Fold up the lid along the scores.
32. Apply glue to the top of the four little flaps and press them to the short sides of the lid.
33. Press down a small piece of linen tape to help hold the flaps in place.

Covering the lid:
34. Put the 6¹/2" x 8¹/2" cover paper in front of you, wrong-side up.
35. Apply glue to the top of the lid, around the window. Center it on the cover paper and press down.
36. Abut a ruler to the side of the lid and draw lines extending from each side. Do the same for all four sides. You will now have another tic-tac-toe grid.
37. Draw diagonals across the end squares at the corners closest to the lid. Leave at least ¹/4" between the lid and the corners you will cut. (See the diagram.)
38. Cut along the lines and across the corners, making sure that the cover paper will overlap slightly to cover the lid corners.

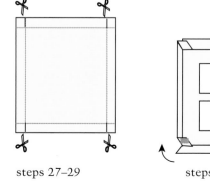

steps 27–29

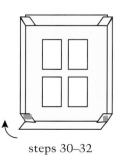

steps 30–32

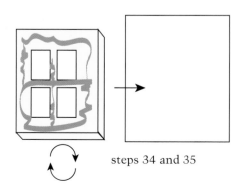

steps 34 and 35

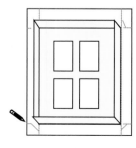

steps 36 and 37

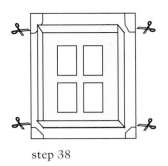
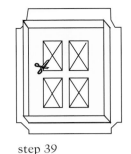
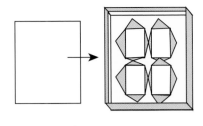

step 38 step 39 step 42

39. Make an "x" with your art knife, across the cover paper just where the window will be. (See the diagram.)

40. Apply glue to each outer flap and press down against the lid. Tuck in the corners as you go.

41. Apply glue to the window flaps and wrap the cover paper around the edges of the window. If you have an unusual shape, you may need to trim the flaps so they will not be visible from the outside.

42. Apply glue to the margin around the window and place the 6¹/₄" x 4¹/₄" Mylar here. Hold in place for a minute or two or put a light weight on top.

For the scenes:
The objects in each scene need to be connected to the sides or top or bottom of the card for this tunnel to work. (See the photograph.)

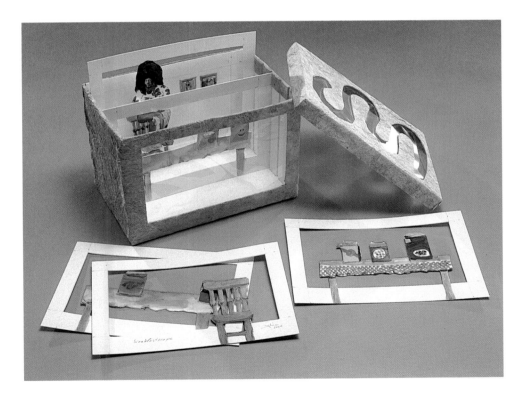

BreakfastScape, detail

Surprise Box, 2000; laser-printed clip art, museum board, Mylar; unique; 6¼" x 5" x 4"

43. Draw a scene on a 4½" x 6¼" piece of paper. Think about the depth of the scene; what is behind something? Try to think of a scene where many things are behind many other things. Draw only the outlines. You will do the details later.

44. Shade the back side of the paper with the side of your pencil.

45. Align the paper with the scene on it with one piece of the 2-ply board. Trace over your lines. Repeat for the remaining five boards.

46. Number your boards lightly from 1–6.

47. Take the first board. What is at the very front of the scene? Draw only this object/character on the first board. Put in all the details.

48. Draw the object that is directly behind the first one on the second board. Repeat for all the boards. Use board number six as the background for the entire scene, such as a back wall, the sky, etc.

49. Take a ruler and pencil and measure a border that is ½" on the top and sides and ¾" from the bottom edge of each scene (except board number six).

50. Make sure that the objects in each scene are touching or overlapping the border on at least one edge.

51. With your art knife, cut out the silhouette of the object, leaving it in contact with the borders. Repeat for all but board number six. Board number six will not be cut. It is the final background.

52. Paint, color or collage the images. Leave the borders white.

53. Arrange the boards in the box. You may need to trim them a bit so they will fit in the grooves.

54. Place the lid on top. You are finished. You may make another set of six cards to change the scene whenever you like.

BOOK QUILT
(SEWING)

Someone asked me how we should display artists' books. I suggested that since it would not be appropriate to frame them, we should have a special spot on our bookshelves reserved for handmade books. But they require more care than the average paperback. And they look good from the front. The problem is how to display them, keep them dust-free, and have them be accessible to our touch at the same time. Archival materials companies sell acrylic cubes for sculptures (or autographed baseballs). Hobby shops and frame stores sell shadowbox frames: deep frames that can hold three-dimensional objects. But the frames open from the back, and they're awkward if you want to handle the book. An ideal spot is a glass-topped table that has drawers; the books could sit open, but you could reach into the drawers to turn the pages or take out the books. Glass-front bookcases are also nice, but expensive. While you are saving up for a large piece of furniture, try making a display quilt.

Val Simonetti had an idea for a postcard quilt; I made one for her in the late 1980s. Today I see wall hangings with pockets everywhere: shower curtains with pockets, displays that hold small stuffed toys, window curtains made of organza with pockets for leaves. It seems logical that we should extend this idea and make a display for handmade books. A local community center or library may be pleased to show books in the quilt since the installation is so simple; you only need a couple of hooks to hold the top dowel. I use clear, thick vinyl for a sturdy display.

All my quilts are too big to make at a table. I spread out on the floor and put on some good music. This project can take several hours or most evenings for a week.

Tools: awl, cardboard, scissors, thimble, thin permanent marker, one or two dowels 1/2" diameter, 36" ruler, T-square, sharp needle with a medium-large eye (some bookbinding needles fit this description)

Materials: clear vinyl 12–14 gauge, various colors of embroidery thread

Book Quilt, 1994; vinyl, embroidery thread; unique; 53½" x 46"

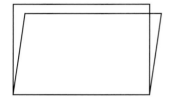

step 1

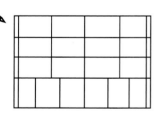

steps 2, 3, and 4

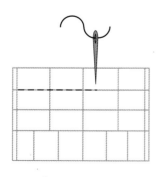

step 5

1. Fold the clear vinyl in half widthwise. Line up the corners. Static should make it stay in this position.

2. Leave a margin on the right and left edges that is about ½".

3. Measure and make small marks with a permanent pen. Pockets should be 5" x 7" if you want the quilt to hold 4" x 6" cards or books. Make 6" x 8" pockets to hold 5" x 7" cards or books. You may want to make some pockets horizontal and some vertical.

4. Begin to connect your marks by placing the ruler just at one mark and lining it up with the one across from it at the opposite end of the vinyl. You will end up with a grid.

5. Using a sharp needle with a medium-large eye threaded with embroidery thread, start sewing in and out along the lines. If you poke holes with an awl first it will be easier to sew. Before you poke the holes, put down a piece or two of cardboard to protect your floor or table. Make holes evenly spaced, ½" apart. It is tedious but may save your fingers.

Note: Don't put any photocopied items in the pockets. Plastic tends to transfer toner from copies, ruining both the photocopies and the inside of the pocket.

Variation: For an intriguing, mysterious display make a smaller version using muslin or other sheer fabric. Fray the ends of the pockets for a textural effect or hem them neatly. Use a sewing machine for book quilts made of fabric.

PAPER MÂCHÉ
(GLUING)

When you think of paper mâché do you think of strips of newspapers dipped in laundry starch? That's what we used when I was a kid. We started with a balloon for the form or skeleton, then wrapped the wet strips around the balloon. Once dry, we could poke a pin into the paper ball and the balloon would deflate, leaving the paper ball intact. We made animals out of these forms and painted them with poster paint.

Fine artists use a version of paper mâché; Edward Hutchins used paper mâché for his scroll-book-within-a-frog called *Lunch!* I have had success with strips of mulberry paper dipped in wheat paste and painted with acrylics. Unlike polymer clay, paper mâché doesn't break. Make animals holding books like Ed did, or make boxes. I use museum board and self-adhesive linen tape to make the framework. The paper mâché stands up to lots of layers of paint for a very artistic, handmade look like this pair of *Artist's Dice*. I put beads inside some house-shaped boxes and called the finished pieces *Noises in the House.* (Photo on page 156.)

You can also use metal or glass bowls for the outer form. Before you begin, spray the bowl with a silicone-release or vegetable cooking spray or put a layer of plastic wrap over it. You can sand the paper bowl when it is dry. Paint it with acrylics, if you like. Make a book about eating or food and put it inside the finished paper mâché bowl.

Artist's Dice, 1997; acrylics, museum board, paper mâché; 2¹/₂" x 2" x 2"

CHAPTER 10

MATERIALS AND METHODS

You can use ordinary materials that you probably already have at home to make interesting books. Experiment and play. Later, if you want to invest in special paper, you will know what you are looking for based on your experiments. Is the paper too stiff? Is it too translucent? Does it rip too easily? Does the color run when you try to paint on it? You'll know what you want after your hands have worked with what you have. The following reference guide can help you choose suitable materials for your projects. It also includes basic stitches, knots, and bindings. The final section covers exhibiting and selling your book art projects.

ADHESIVES

Often a very specific type of adhesive is needed for a project. For the structures in this book you will need at least two different kinds of adhesive: PVA (polyvinyl acetate, which is a white glue) and wheat paste.

The type of glue that is sold for bookbinding is much better than the watered-down version that is sold in the grocery store. A good PVA glue dries rapidly (as quickly as within five minutes) and becomes clear and flexible. School glues tend to take much longer to dry and become brittle over time. I don't recommend any substitutions for PVA.

When you work with wheat paste you have a chance to reposition your work before it hardens forever. This is especially useful when you are covering boards for a hardcover book. Add wheat paste powder to clean (or distilled) water in small amounts, stirring well after each addition. Keep adding powder until the mixture is medium-thick but can still be stirred. After thirty min-

Coriander Reisbord: *Unspeakable*, 1998; Japanese paper and paste, accordion fold, eighteen panels; unique; 5³/₈" x 7"

utes the paste will thicken even more. It is too thick if it stands up on a plate by itself. You can thin it back down and strain it if it is too lumpy. A cooked paste can be made from one part flour and four parts water. Use a wire whisk and stir it constantly. Pastes keep in a sealed plastic container in the refrigerator for about two weeks. I like to mix the paste with PVA so I can have both the benefits of a longer working time from the paste and the tackiness and flexibility of the PVA. Don't cook or heat the PVA, and keep it out of your cooking pots or dishes.

For some projects a glue stick will be good enough. If you have a large area to cover, you might try the kind of commercial "stick-flat" paste that is pre-made; it functions like glue stick. You will need a brush to apply it. It is generally not archival.

I like using a flat-bottomed stencil brush to apply adhesives since the bristles are short and I can spread the adhesives evenly. Wash your brush or soak it immediately after use, especially when working with PVA. If you only need small amounts of adhesive, you might use a small piece of heavy cardboard to spread it.

When you use adhesives, always decant your adhesive from a larger container to a smaller "working" container or paper plate. Dipping a brush into the adhesive brings in fibers that will encourage undesirable mold to grow in the main batch.

Self-adhesive linen tape, sold in framing departments of art-supply stores, is the only tape you will be able to use on your books with good results. It is usually sold in a roll of 400". Other tapes will yellow, crack, flake, and leave a residue.

In addition to making book art, Coriander Reisbord repairs books professionally. She is familiar with many kinds of papers, adhesives, and restoration techniques that she uses in her art as well as in her job.

Coriander Reisbord: *Defensive Book*, 1993; letterpress, paper, pins, long stitch (separate pamphlets) through one endsheet; edition of 15; 5³/₄" x 7¹/₄"

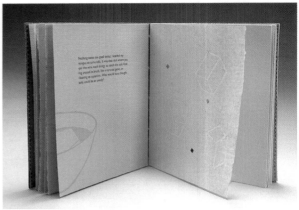

Left: Coriander Reisbord: *Quick Visit*, 1992; letterpress, handmade and commercially made papers, linoleum cuts, silk cover, long stitch through endsheets (separate pamphlets through one piece of paper); 5³/₄" x 6³/₈"
Right: Coriander Reisbord: *Quick Visit*, open

"*Unspeakable* was made by laminating three sheets of Japanese paper together with wheat starch paste. The papers are *sekishu* (thicker; the inner piece) and *gasenshi* (thinner; the two outer pieces); the square I cut out of the middle of the *sekishu* is what's folded up floating in the middle. The panels are hinged together with strips of *gasenshi*, glued down with PVA. I used the thinner paper to get a hinge that would be very flexible, and the PVA to make the *gasenshi* a little stronger.

"This book is about secrets, and trying to have it both ways: the relief of telling one's shameful secrets, without the shame of people knowing what they are. I like that the secrets are inside the pages, underneath the surface: their existence is revealed but not their substance.

"I made *Defensive Book* by laminating text-weight printmaking papers together over pins. I used wheat starch paste for the laminating, and printed the text onto the sheets before I laminated them. I pressed the sheets in a nipping press between pieces of closed-cell foam sleeping-bag pad, so that the paper would be molded around the pins as sharply as possible. The pages get smaller as you move through the book, and the pins get more numerous.

"I tried to show that if you try to follow all the rules for self-protection, you end up living an intolerably constricted life. The text was lifted from a university pamphlet on safety for female students.

"*Quick Visit* is letterpress printed, with linoleum-block illustrations and illustrations made with watermarks. The story tells about a short visit I made to friends in Japan. The binding was done for an exhibition of fine bindings; I wanted something that would be fancy, but also Japanese. I do not like Japanese-style bindings put onto books made of Western-style paper! So I used kimono fabric, and mounted it on paper to use it as book cloth. I made two covers, identical but of two different fabrics, and I sewed the three signatures of the text block through the inner one, and then glued the outer one to it. I left the spine free, like a hollow-back book. Then I used a sewing machine without any thread in it to punch the holes all around the edge, which I retraced with thick colored thread by hand."

CORIANDER REISBORD

Keeping the Paper Flat

You will need a way to press the book or papers flat while the adhesive dries. Some bookbinders use a very heavy piece of equipment called a nipping press. I use several smooth-sided Masonite boards that are 11" x 14" each. Make a book press as follows: one Masonite board, one sheet of waxed paper, the project, one sheet of waxed paper, one Masonite board. If you have more than one project, you can keep stacking them up like so many sandwiches. Make sure you always have waxed paper between the project and the boards. Also use waxed paper between pages of your book so that the pages won't stick together. Put heavy books (like dictionaries) or bricks on top of the boards.

Mounting Paper

There may be times when you have a drawing or small separate image or text that you would like to include in your finished book. You can mount this drawing onto a heavier book page most easily with a glue stick, since the paper won't warp when the adhesive dries. Spray adhesives do cause paper to warp and bubble over time, and I don't recommend them. When glue is applied to only one side of a paper, the paper tends to pull or warp. For best results, apply glue and paper to both sides of the heavier backing paper or "tip in" the drawing by putting small, thin spots of glue at the corners or edges only. Wheat paste is too wet for tipping in.

To make the drawing into a card for the card-file book or other small project, use a thin coat of PVA. Apply the PVA to the back of your drawing, then smooth the drawing onto the heavier paper. Put the now-laminated papers between two sheets of waxed paper and under a heavy book or some wooden or Masonite boards with weights on top. Don't try to mount a picture onto a piece of heavier paper or board that is exactly the same size. It is much easier if you use a piece of heavier paper that is larger than your picture and then trim it to size when it is completely dry.

Backing Cloth

To use cloth to cover a board you must first adhere the cloth to a sheet of a strong, lightweight paper. The process of "backing" cloth is similar to that of mounting paper except that you use wheat paste only. The paste should be a bit runny, so that it spreads slowly when put on a paper plate. It should be without lumps. Use a strainer, if necessary, to get rid of the lumps.

I like using mulberry paper for my backing sheet since it is thin but strong. Use only wheat paste. PVA dries too quickly and if you get any spots of glue on the cloth they are nearly impossible to wipe off.

1. Cut the cloth so that it is slightly smaller than the paper.
2. Put the cloth face down on the table.
3. Mist the cloth lightly with water and smooth it out on your work surface.
4. Apply paste to the paper.

5. Center and smooth the cloth face up onto the paper, rubbing out any bubbles that may occur.

6. You can let it air-dry or you can cover it with waxed paper and put wooden boards and weights on top. Let it dry at least overnight.

Variation: If you have a smooth, clean work surface that you don't need to use for a day, leave the misted cloth on the table. After applying paste to the paper, turn the paper over and smooth it onto the cloth. Let it dry on the table. It will remain flat this way. Peel it off the table when dry.

PAPER

Paper Weights

Lightweight papers: Papers in this group fold, wrinkle, and tear easily. They are often somewhat translucent. Examples include 20–24 lb. bond paper (typing, laser writer, or copy paper), glassine, newsprint, origami paper, and Asian papers such as mulberry paper.

Medium-weight papers: These can be folded repeatedly. They can accept layers of drawing. They are opaque. A sheet of this paper will not tear easily if a hole is cut in it. Examples include the paper of a manila envelope, all-cotton resumé paper, glossy magazine covers, and decorative papers that you cannot see through.

Heavy-weight papers: These hold up well to paint and gesso and repeated erasings. Examples include printmaking paper, cover stock, index cards, and watercolor paper.

2-ply board: This is a board that is made of two layers of thick paper. Two-ply museum board is preferred for archival use, since it is 100% cotton and does not turn yellow or show spots over time. For non-archival use, you can substitute cardboard that is the thickness of the cardboard used for cereal boxes.

4-ply board: This is a stiff board that is made of four layers of thick paper. Museum board is archival and is available in 4-ply thickness. Mat board and illustration board are non-archival 4-ply boards that are available in a wide variety of colors.

Paper Grain

Almost all papers have a grain, or direction in which they can be folded or torn most easily. Test the grain by gently attempting to fold the paper both horizontally and vertically. The grain runs parallel to the easiest fold. Books generally need to have the grain of the paper running parallel to the spine. If

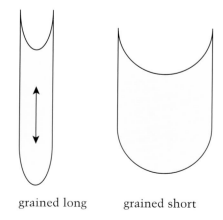

grained long   grained short

the paper has no distinguishable grain, it is fine to use it either way. Hand-made papers often have no grain. Grained short means that the grain runs parallel to the shortest side of the paper. Grained long means the grain runs parallel to the longest side of the paper.

MOCK-UPS

Once you decide what to include in your next book, make a mock-up. Create the structure for your book out of scratch paper and tape it together. Number the pages. If you have text, write it, type it, or print it out on a single sheet of paper. Look through the text and draw lines between sections that could stand alone on a page. When you are satisfied with the section breaks, number these sections in pencil. Cut them apart and begin taping them to the pages in your mock-up. Leave room at the beginning for a title page and possibly a page in the back for a colophon.

The mock-up can be just as interesting as the final project. In 1976, Dieter Roth made a wonderful-looking book from paper and taped-on images called *Collected Works, Volume 17: 246 Little Clouds.* The "little clouds" in the title refer to the taped-on images and the shadows they cast on the pages. If you want your mock-up to be archival, use only self-adhesive linen tape.

MEASURING, SCORING, CUTTING

Use a good ruler that has clear numbers and small increments (16ths or millimeters). When measuring, mark your work with a sharp pencil only. Erase this mark later, if necessary. A dull pencil leaves a wide mark that makes errors in measuring more likely.

To find the center of odd-sized paper without getting a math headache, you might invest in a center-finding ruler. It has the conventional marks on one edge and a zero in the center of the other long edge; the inch marks move out toward the short edges.

Templates

Making a template is helpful if you are making an edition. By using a template you don't need to measure every time you want to make a window. You can also use the template for a placement guide: you may want a small collage on the front cover of every book in exactly the same place. Draw light pencil lines that can be erased later. White plastic erasers work best. Don't try using the pink ones, they often leave marks.

1. Use a sturdy, non-corrugated cardboard the same size as your page.
2. Measure precisely where you want the window.

3. Use an art knife and metal ruler to cut out the hole.

4. Put sturdy plastic tape around the edges of the opening, if you desire. Use this template only for drawing! Do not use it as a cutting guide.

5. With pencil, draw through the template to your project where you want the hole.

6. Use an art knife against a metal ruler to cut the window.

Making a Jig for Measuring and Poking Holes

You can make holes that are evenly spaced without using a ruler. To measure for an odd number of holes, get a strip of paper the same height as the book on which you are working and make a jig.

For three holes:

1. Fold the paper in half widthwise.

2. Keep it folded, then fold one end so that it is touching the middle fold.

3. Turn the paper over.

4. Fold up the other end so that it is aligned with the first end.

5. Open.

6. Fold in half lengthwise.

7. Nest this jig in the very center fold of the pages you want to sew (or wrap around the left edge for a sidebound book).

8. Poke the holes.

9. Remove the jig.

For five holes:

1. Fold the paper in half widthwise. Open.

2. Fold up one of the short ends so that the edge of the paper is halfway between the new bottom fold and the middle fold.

3. Keep this new flap folded. Reverse the middle fold from a valley to a peak fold.

4. Turn the paper over. Fold up the other end so that it is aligned with the first end.

5. Open the middle fold again.

6. Bring the bottom fold up to the middle fold. Crease.

7. Bring the top fold down to the middle fold. Crease.

8. Open completely.

9. Fold in half lengthwise.

step 1

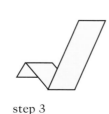

step 2

step 4

step 6

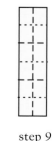

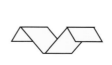

step 2   step 3   step 4   step 6   step 9

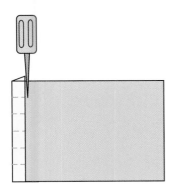

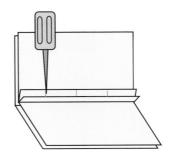

Five holes for large sidebound book   Three holes in the center fold

Poking the holes:
Use a piece of cardboard to protect your work surface. Clip your pages open and together, with the jig in the center fold of the pages you want to sew or wrapped around the left edge of a sidebound book. Put the pages on your work surface. Hold the awl with your thumb on top of the handle. Push down the awl into the places where the folds of the jig intersect. If you keep the pages clipped, you are now ready to sew your project together.

Scoring

When your paper is stiff, a good way to produce a clean fold is to score or indent the paper first. Place a wood or metal ruler next to the line you want to fold. With your thumbnail, a bone folder, or a butter knife press a line into the paper. Keep the ruler in place and use it to help you fold the paper up against it. Remove the ruler and make a firm crease by smoothing the paper with your hands or a bone folder. For very thick paper only, such as museum board or cardboard, you may need to make a very light cut instead of a score by using an art knife. Since you have weakened the board, cover it afterward with another material such as cloth or paper.

Cutting

Always protect your work surface and the sharpness of your art knife by cutting on top of cardboard or a self-healing cutting mat. The good thing about the mat is that you can reuse it for many years. Cardboard is inexpensive, but if you reuse it, the previous cuts in the cardboard will interfere with future cuts.

Keep a good stock of fresh knife blades on hand. A dull knife can ruin a project. Dull knives can be more dangerous than sharp ones.

Cut against a metal or metal-edged ruler only. Do not attempt freehand cuts. Keep your fingers behind the edge of the ruler. I find it easier to maintain a straight cut and even pressure if I am standing up while I cut.

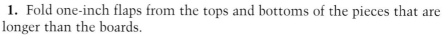

FOLDS
Accordion fold

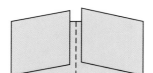

step 2

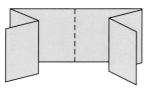

step 3

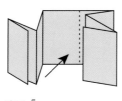

step 5

To make an accordion with eight segments:
1. Fold the paper in half widthwise. Open.
2. Fold the ends to the middle fold, one end at a time.
3. Fold the ends back to the new folds, making sure they are aligned.
4. Turn the paper over, keeping everything folded.
5. Align the folded ends with the middle fold; crease. You should now have an accordion with alternating peak and valley folds.

To make an accordion with sixteen segments:
Follow steps 1 and 2 above. Open. Make four more valley folds by matching each folded edge and each of the two ends to its neighboring fold. Turn the paper over. Start from one end and match the end to its neighboring fold. Continue until the paper is completely folded, alternating peak and valley folds.

Wrapped Hard Cover

Materials: two equal-sized pieces of 2-ply or 4-ply museum board, two sheets of medium-weight paper the same width as the boards and 2" longer than the height, grained short, two sheets of medium-weight paper the same height as the boards and 2" wider, grained short

1. Fold one-inch flaps from the tops and bottoms of the pieces that are longer than the boards.
2. Fold one-inch flaps from the right and left edges of the pieces that are wider than the boards.
3. Take one board and wrap one of the wider pieces around it.

step 1

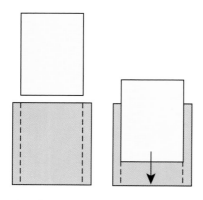

step 2

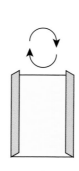

step 4

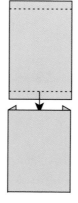

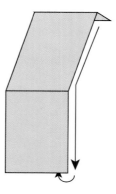

step 5

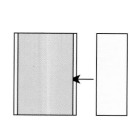

step 7

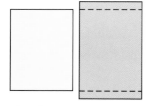

Datebook, 1989; rubber stamps, collage, pop-up; wrapped hard cover; unique; 6" x 7³/8" x 1¹/4"

4. Turn the wrapped board over.

5. Tuck the sides of the longer paper into the first paper, completely covering the board.

6. Repeat steps 3–5 for the second board.

7. Take one end of your book and tuck it into the cover along the open side. Repeat for the other end and the second cover.

Optional: You can make a spine by using a strip of paper the same height as the boards. Fold the strip in half or thirds. Tuck one end into the side of one wrapped cover. Repeat for the other end.

SEWING, KNOTS, AND STITCHES

For best results, use thread or string that does not break or stretch when you pull hard. Test a piece before you start. Linen or waxed linen works well; embroidery thread or polyester-wrapped cotton is usually fine. Yarn or cotton thread will likely break. Silk can be slippery. To reduce slipperiness and to add strength and manageability to any thread, use your fingers to draw the thread across a small cake of beeswax.

Use a needle that has an eye large enough for the thread you are using. Bookbinding needles have an average-size eye and are sturdy and sharp enough to poke holes in lightweight paper as well. You may be able to get a bookbinding needle in a package of "repair needles" sold at grocery, drug, or fabric stores. Or purchase one at a bookbinding supply shop. A variety of needles is good to have on hand.

Before you begin to sew, clamp your pages together with a binder clip. To prevent your book pages from becoming dented by the clip, insert a pad between the clip and the pages. Make a pad by folding one sheet of scrap paper into several thicknesses. Sandwich the book pages between the pad. Put the clip over the pad, holding the pad and the pages together. When you are done sewing, remove the clip and the pad. (While none of the diagrams in this book actually show the pad, any time a clip is shown a pad is indicated as well.)

Square Knot

Take note of the string that is first on your right; this is the string that does all the work.

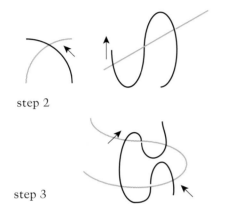

step 2

step 3

1. Hold one piece of string in your right hand, the other piece in your left hand.
2. Cross the right piece over the left piece and back under the left piece.
3. Now the piece that was originally in your right hand is in your left hand. Cross the (now left) piece over the (now right) piece and back under the (now right piece).
4. Pull to tighten.

Overhand Knot

1. Hold both ends of the string in one palm.
2. Wrap the string over all your fingers and across the piece in your palm.
3. Slip your fingers out and put the ends through the loop.

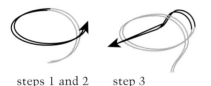

steps 1 and 2   step 3

Kettle Stitch or Half-Hitch Knot

You will need this knot for some of the books with more than two signatures.

1. Work on the outside of the book at the last hole (either head or tail). Take the threaded needle from the outside underneath the stitch that links the two preceding signatures.
2. Before you pull the thread all the way through, cross the needle over to make a loop.
3. Now take the needle back through the loop of thread, holding the knot close to the book as you pull it gently and tighten it firmly.

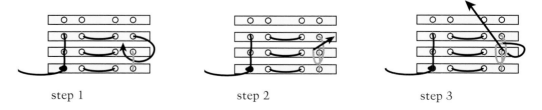

step 1   step 2   step 3

Single Signature

Use this three-hole binding for a small pamphlet or if you are adding signatures to an accordion-based structure.

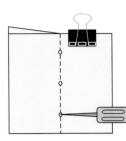

steps 1 and 2

1. Fold papers in half with the grain running parallel to the fold.
2. Nest the papers inside each other with the folds aligned.
3. Clamp the papers together with a binder clip over a protective pad.
4. With an awl or your needle, poke three holes in the fold, at even intervals, leaving at least one half inch from each end.

Sewing pattern with three holes:
5. Start with the middle hole.
6. Go back out one end hole.
7. Skip the middle and make a long stitch to the other end hole.
8. Come back through the middle, and tie a square knot around the long stitch. It should look like two stitches now.

step 3   step 4

Sewing pattern with five holes for a larger book:

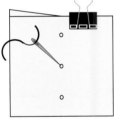

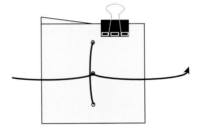

step 5   step 6   steps 7 and 8   step 8

I don't like to leave more than two inches between holes. Use more than three holes if your book is very tall. You can use any uneven number. This example uses five holes.

1. Poke five holes down the fold, with no holes closer than one half inch from the head and tail.
2. Start at the middle hole, as for the pamphlet.
3. Sew a running stitch (alternating in and out) down to the tail and back up toward the middle again.
4. Stop when you get to the hole immediately neighboring the middle hole.

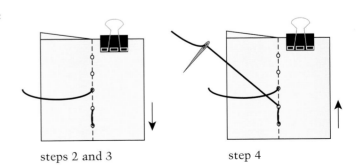

steps 2 and 3   step 4

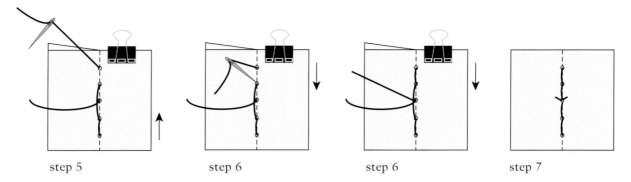

step 5   step 6   step 6   step 7

5. Skip the middle hole and sew up to the head.
6. Sew back down and come out the middle hole.
7. Tie off in a square knot the two ends of thread straddling the long stitch. It should look like two stitches now.

Hem Stitch

1. Thread the needle and knot the end.
2. Take your needle into the cloth, so that the knot will be hidden inside, under one folded layer of cloth as you sew up the outside.
3. Make a tiny stitch up through the folded layers of one side of the opening.
4. Go into the folded layers of the other side parallel to the first hole and immediately take your needle diagonally through the second layers and up through the first layers about $1/8$"–$1/4$" from the first hole.
5. Repeat steps 1–4 until you get to the end of the edges you are sewing together.
6. Make a knot that will hide inside the folds by taking your needle through the cloth. Then make a loop, take your needle through the loop, and tighten the knot.
7. Trim the end closely.

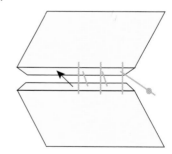

steps 1–4

Quilter's Binding

Use this binding for cloth books when you want a neat, finished appearance. You will need four strips of cloth, one to two inches wide, for the binding for each page. Two strips should be the same length as your page. Two strips should be about two inches longer than the width of your page. Although it takes a bit of time to sew the quilter's binding, I find it somehow soothing and satisfying to do it.

1. Sandwich your cloth and craft and quilting fleece as you want it to appear: all right sides facing out and visible. Pin it together.

2. If your cloth book is more than 8" you will probably want to quilt it. This means you need to sew small knots every few inches by hand, or machine-stitch a pattern (it could just be a square frame just inside the edges of the page).

3. Iron the strips folded in half lengthwise to make them narrower.

4. Pin one strip to the edge of your page; then open the end at the edge of the open edge of the page. Pin it every two inches or so.

5. Machine-sew a $1/4$" hem, attaching the strip to the page, taking the pins out as you go.

6. Take the folded edge of the strip and wrap it over the open edge of the page. Pull the folded edge gently until it covers the machine stitching on the reverse side.

7. Hand-sew this folded edge with a hem stitch. Continue to pull the fold over the stitching until you have completed this side.

8. Trim the ends of the binding to make it even with the page.

9. Repeat steps 4–8 for the *parallel* edge.

10. Fold in 1" from one end of the third strip of binding.

11. Pin this folded end exactly to the corner, the long open edge corresponding to the open edge of the page. Continue to pin the binding strip every two inches.

12. Machine-sew a $1/4$" hem, attaching the third strip to the page, taking the pins out as you go until you get to one inch from the end.

13. Fold in 1" from the end and sew it down.

14. Take the folded edge of the strip and wrap it over the open edge of the page. Pull the folded edge gently until it covers the machine stitching on the reverse side.

15. Hand-sew this folded edge with a hem stitch. Continue to pull the fold over the stitching until you have completed this side.

16. Repeat steps 10–15 for the fourth strip and edge.

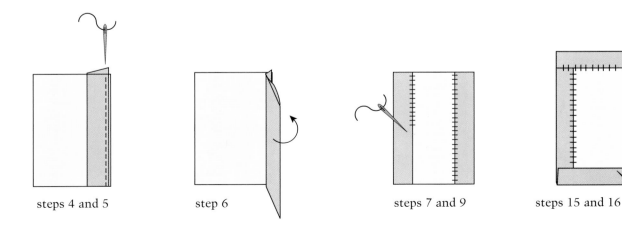

steps 4 and 5   step 6   steps 7 and 9   steps 15 and 16

COVERS AND DUST JACKETS

Spray Coating

If I wrap boards with a soft, thin paper to make a hardcover book, I occasionally spray the finished book front and back with an acrylic spray coating. In reality, I try to avoid doing this because it smells so bad and is terribly hazardous. If you use the spray, put down some newspaper underneath your book and spray the book out of doors only. For further protection for yourself, wear a mask. Then, if you are able, let the book dry somewhere far away. It may take a few weeks before the smell is completely gone, but you have added a protective layer that may be worth it; you can still feel the texture of the paper.

If you use colored pencils or pastels you can use a mist made especially to hold the pigments to the paper. Look for it with the chalk pastels or with the other spray coatings in an art supply store. This, too, carries many health warnings and should only be used outside.

Mylar

If the feel of the book is not as important as protecting it completely, make a dust jacket out of thin Mylar. Mylar is the key word here; acetate tears, yellows, and eventually becomes brittle. Mylar is what those in the paper industry call "dimensionally stable." It doesn't change over time; it keeps its clarity and stays sturdy. If the shininess doesn't bother you, Mylar is the best way to protect your book.

Paper or Mylar Dust Jacket

Your local bookstore has books bound in cloth, but they all have paper dust jackets. Usually the cloth and the jacket are related by color or type style. Add an extra dimension to your artwork by incorporating a paper dust jacket into your design. The paper must be sturdy and able to withstand handling. Remember, too, that light colors show dirt. (Try not to make an all-white dust jacket. Your readers will be afraid to touch it.) For additional inspiration, read the book *Jackets Required*, by Steven Heller and Seymour Chwast, for an illustrated history of American book jacket design from 1920 to 1950.

To make a Mylar or paper dust jacket, first purchase a sheet of Mylar or paper from your local art supply store. Mylar is often kept in the paper department and sold by the sheet (which may be 18" x 24" in size). Measure your book.

1. Cut your Mylar so that it is exactly the same height as your book but approximately twice as long as the book when it is open. The added length will be the front and back flaps, and you may make them as long or as short

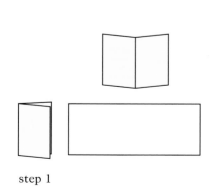

step 1

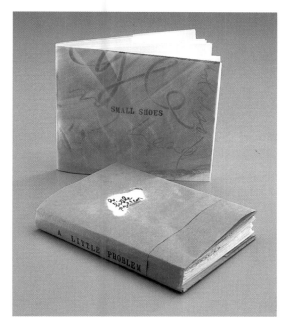

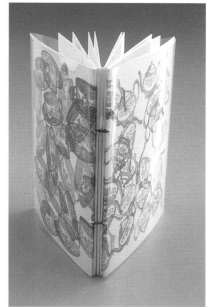

Left: Dust jacket ideas: *Small Shoes,* 2000; glassine cover; 4^1/$_4$" x 3^1/$_4$". *A Little Problem,* 2000; torn bag cover; 3" x 4^1/$_4$"
Right: *Tea,* 2000; sample Mylar dust jacket over rubber-stamped images; linked-stitch binding; 4^1/$_4$" x 5^1/$_2$" x ^{3}/$_8$"

as you like. I like it better if the flaps are each *at least* half the size of the cover. If they are too short, they pop off when the book is opened.

 2. Find the middle of the Mylar. Measure and score a tiny mark on the Mylar with your thumbnail or a bone folder (or make a groove with a pencil). If your book has a spine piece, measure it. Use a centering ruler or, for example, if your spine is ^{1}/$_2$", measure ^{1}/$_4$" on either side of the center mark.

 3. Measure ^{1}/$_4$" on either side of the center score/groove on the Mylar. Make two long scores, one at each measurement, parallel to the short side of the Mylar.

 4. From this score line, measure (toward the closest edge from each score) the same width as the width of your book. If your book is a hardcover book, add ^{1}/$_8$" to the measurement. Make another score line here. The added measurement will allow the book to flex when it is opened; the soft-cover dust jacket should not be too tight.

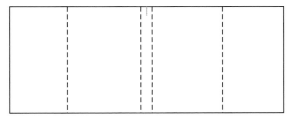

steps 2–4

Glued Hard Covers

You will need a way to press the book flat when you make hard covers. Some bookbinders use a nipping press. I have some smooth-sided Masonite boards that are about 11" x 14" each that I put on top of my projects. On top of the boards I put heavy books or a couple of bricks.

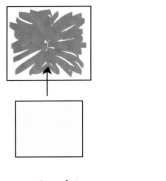

steps 3 and 4

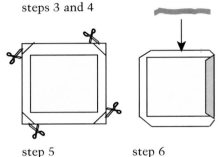

step 5   step 6

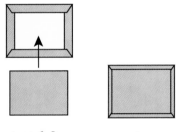

steps 6–8   step 8

Materials and tools needed: waxed paper, old magazines for scrap paper, scissors, PVA and wheat paste mixture (about 50/50), glue brush or piece of stiff board to spread the glue, ruler, pencil, bone folder or wooden spoon to smooth the adhered papers, and 4-ply museum board, the outer covering paper and the inner paper (endsheets). A $^3/_{16}$" metal spacing bar, purchased from a hardware store, is handy but not mandatory.

To cover separate boards

1. Cover your work surface with pages from the magazine, giving yourself a few layers. You will be discarding these layers as they get messy.
2. Arrange your outer cover paper in front of you, wrong-side up.
3. Spread adhesive evenly on your paper with a brush or piece of board, working from the center outward. Discard one layer of scrap paper to give yourself a clean surface.
4. Center a piece of board on the tacky outer paper. Press down.
5. Cut off the corners of the outer paper, leaving at least the thickness of the board as a margin between the board and the diagonal you will cut. Turn the corners over and stick them down to your scrap paper as you go. Discard the scrap paper.
6. Apply more glue to the flaps, if necessary. Fold and smooth down each flap, in any order. Give the paper a little push in with your thumbnail when you are at the corners, so that the corner tips of the board will be completely covered and the cover paper doesn't stick out.
7. Apply adhesive to the back of the inner cover paper.
8. Center the inner cover paper and press it into place. Smooth it down.
9. Place between two sheets of waxed paper, under wooden boards with a weight on top. Let dry at least overnight, possibly for a week if weather conditions are cold or damp.

To cover two boards and a spine piece

1. Spread magazines over your work surface.
2. Put the cover paper wrong-side up. Find the center and mark it with a pencil, or fold the paper in half.
3. Apply glue/paste to the center of the cover paper; press down the spine here.
4. Spread glue/paste on one half the cover paper.

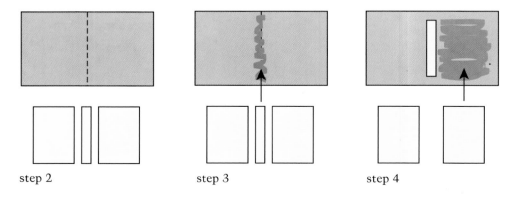

step 2   step 3   step 4

5. Put a spacing bar next to the spine or measure $^3/16"$. Place the board next to the spacing bar or press into place $^3/16"$ from the spine. Remove the spacing bar.

6. Spread glue/paste on the other half of the cover paper.

7. Use the spacing bar again or measure $^3/16"$ the way you did in step 5. Press the second board into place. Remove the spacing bar.

8. Cut diagonals across the corners, leaving a margin before you cut the diagonal.

9. Apply glue/paste to the edges one at a time, in any order, and fold down the edges.

10. Remove the project to a clean work surface. With waxed paper between the bone folder and the project, rub down the adhered paper.

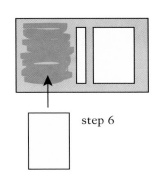

step 6

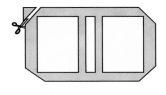

steps 7 and 8

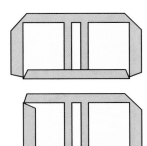

step 9

To attach hard covers

11. Get new scrap paper. Open the first page of the signature and put it on top of the scrap paper, leaving the rest of the signature closed. Apply glue evenly in a fanlike manner only to the back of this paper.

12. Pick up the book block, taking care not to get glue on the rest of the book. The front and back boards for your book will be approximately $^1/4"$–$^1/2"$ larger than your book block. Arrange the now-sticky endsheet on the covered boards so it has a border of $^1/8"$–$^1/4"$ around it.

13. Rub down the sheet with a bone folder. Put a piece of waxed paper between the newly glued sheet and the rest of the book block. Close the book and face it to the left.

14. Open the back cover. The rest of the book block should be closed on the left.

15. Put a piece of scrap paper between the last sheet and the rest of the book block. Apply glue to the back of the last sheet. Remove the scrap paper.

16. You may need to close the book slightly (possibly to a 45-degree angle) to obtain the same margins ($^1/8"$–$^1/4"$, whatever border you chose in step 12) as the front inner cover. Press the sticky sheet down onto the back board.

17. Over waxed paper, rub down with the bone folder.

18. Place waxed paper between the newly glued sheet and the rest of the book block. Close the book.

19. Place between waxed paper and Masonite boards. Put a heavy weight on top. Let the project dry overnight.

step 11

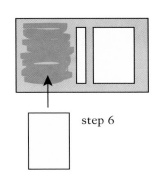

step 12

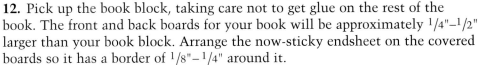

step 13

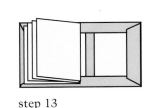

steps 13–15

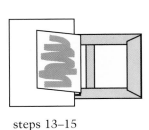

step 16

To cover boards with a spine piece for a sidebound book

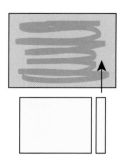

steps 3 and 4

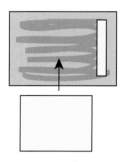

steps 4 and 5

1. Cover your work surface with pages from a magazine, giving yourself a few layers. You will be discarding these layers as they get messy.

2. Arrange one outer cover paper in front of you horizontally, wrong-side up.

3. Spread adhesive evenly on your paper with a brush or piece of board, working from the center outward. Discard one layer of scrap paper to give yourself a clean surface.

4. For the front cover, place a spine strip approximately 1" from the right edge of the paper. Press down.

5. Leave approximately $3/16$" (you can use a $3/16$" spacing bar as a guide; take it out before wrapping the boards) and place one of the larger, main cover boards, aligned with the spine strip.

6. Cut diagonals at the corners, leaving a slight margin. Don't cut right up to the edge of the board. Remove the triangles.

7. Apply more glue, if necessary. Fold the edges of the paper over the boards. Move the project to a clean surface.

8. Place the endsheet wrong-side up on a second piece of scrap paper. Apply glue completely to the edges.

9. Carefully pick up this endsheet and center it on the covered boards. Press and rub down.

10. Repeat for the second board.

11. Place covers between two pieces of waxed paper and put these between Masonite boards. Put the books or bricks on top. Let the covers press flat at least overnight, preferably for a few days.

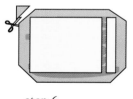

step 6

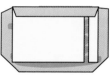

step 7

step 7

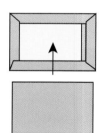

steps 8 and 9

Note: If your front cover paper has a title or other ornamentation, remember that while you are working, you will adhere the boards with the title strip on the right for this front cover. When it is finished and you turn it over, the spine strip will be correctly on the left, assuming you are making a book that reads from left to right. See diagram.

PARTS OF A BOOK

The standard sequence of pages in a book can also be found in *The Chicago Manual of Style* or Adrian Wilson's *The Design of Books*. They also contain chapters regarding design and typography, papermaking and bookmaking.

While it is not necessary to follow this order, knowing the basics may be helpful.

Endpapers (decorative, reflecting the colors and mood of the contents)
Blank sheets (a pause before entering the book; gives room if the book needs to be rebound)
Bastard title (also referred to as the half title; just the title—no author's name or publisher)
Frontispiece (image)
Title page (title, author, publisher)
Copyright (usually on the back of the title page; in the United States a "c" with a circle around it, the year, and author's/illustrator's name follows; for full protection internationally add "all rights reserved")
Dedication
Foreword
Preface
Contents
Introduction
Text
Appendix
Bibliography
Colophon (description of how the book was made: media used, typefaces, paper or other materials, anything else you want to add about the creation of the book)
Blank sheets
Endpapers

The list of ordered pages does not take into account the rhythm or pacing of the book and the sequence of the images and text, which are very important to the making of a thought-provoking, interesting book.

Recto/Verso

The right (correct) side of the page is called the *recto*. In a codex, or book with signatures, the recto is the right-hand page when you open the book. The back or opposite (versus) side is called the *verso*. This is the left-hand page. Many books have a standard, nondramatic format; the poem or words are on the recto, the illustrations are on the verso (or vice versa). To break up the monotony of the pacing, to add interest and surprise, use the recto for some of the images and the verso for some of the words.

Other Terms

Head: the top edge of the book
Tail: the bottom edge of the book
Fore edge: the edge that opens
Spine: the side opposite from the edge that opens

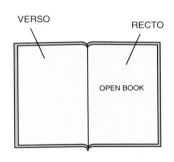

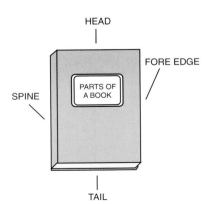

THE BUSINESS OF BOOK ART

Collections

Libraries around the world collect book art. It is often housed in the Rare Books or Special Collections departments. Many universities have classes related to the book arts, and these classes visit the libraries frequently to get ideas. Behind the institutional wall are the teachers and librarians who are excited by these books. Ask to see the special collections in your public library or local college.

If you travel, take books with you in a decorative box or portfolio. Call up Special Collections librarians and make appointments to show your work. Librarians I've met love meeting the artists and are more likely to buy work directly from the maker.

Accessories

Business cards. It is good to have a business card so that potential clients can contact you easily. Make it legible. Your art is important, but the information is more important. Quick-printing shops often have deals that will get you 500–1000 inexpensive cards. As an alternative to 500 cards, you could make just a few cards by hand: you may only want fifty cards if your area code or zip code will be changing in the near future. You may also get tired of the design on 500 cards.

Slides. If you intend to show your book art, you will need professional-quality slides of your work. A plain background is best. Have duplicates made and keep a set for yourself. Label them with your name, the title of the work, the date completed, dimensions, and media used.

Postcards. For professional-looking publicity, get full-color postcards made from a slide of your work. This service is often listed in art magazines. Include these cards in your mailings or as your stationery.

Catalog. Having a catalog shows that you are serious about your work. When you have created several books, make a catalog. Use photographs of the books: most people prefer looking at a picture to reading a long description. When you write descriptions of your books, think about who will read them. Be appealing, accurate, and descriptive in a few sentences.

Subscriptions and Discounts

Sometimes presses offer subscriptions to encourage people to buy their books. The subscriber may get a 20% discount on all books produced annually if s/he has placed a standing order. Discounts may be available to those buyers who prepay. You can send out a coupon with your mailing. Be sure to include an expiration date. If you are too generous with your discount, you may undercut the bookstores and galleries that sell your work. Lowering the price of a book after it has been available for a while frustrates those who have already bought your book; instead of lowering your price, try to offer prospective customers something not available in the stores.

People love the idea of lots of books appearing in their mailboxes. Plan a series that includes three books for one price. Advertise this subscription by using your mailing list. If it sounds appealing, people may try it.

The Business of Collaborating

Even professional artists may wonder how to divide the profits from a collaborative work if they have previously worked alone. A project has many parts. If each person does half the work, it's easy: the profits are split fifty-fifty. What happens when each person does something different? How can you decide what's fair? Make a chart of everything involved in the project that you consider equal. Some categories to consider: design, work (which may be further divided into writing, illustration, printing, binding), funding, sales/marketing. You may be creating a book that has very expensive materials (funding), which include the cost of someone else printing or binding the book. If so, you may not need to include "work" as one of your categories. If you have four categories, each category would be worth 25% of the total income from the book. If you have six categories, each category would be worth 16.66% of the total. Keep the categories as simple as possible.

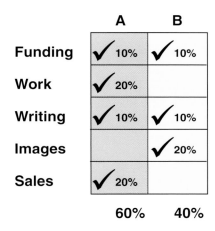

In this example we have five equal categories. Each aspect is worth 20% of the total. Person A pays for half the materials (getting 10% for funding), prints and binds the project (20% for work), does half the writing (another 10%), and agrees to market and sell the book (20%). Total: Person A gets 60%.

Person B pays for half the materials (10%), does half the writing (10%), and makes all the images (20%). Total for Person B: 40% of the selling price.

If you are also dealing with a gallery, you will have to factor in that gallery's percentage. Suppose the gallery gets 50% of the selling price. For a $100 book, that leaves you and your partner with $50 to split, using your calculated percentages. In this example, Person A gets $30 and Person B gets $20.

Galleries and Bookstores

Other people can sell your work for you. But they will likely take 25–50% of the retail price of your book in commission. Think of it as renting space on their shelves. Some galleries deal only with very expensive books or unique books. Others prefer the inexpensive, often photocopied, mass-produced ones. Some galleries like slides, some only want to see the actual work. Write a letter first before you send any books. You may want to send a SASE (self-addressed, stamped envelope). If you send books, include return postage!

The gallery may not want to purchase your book outright but want it "on consignment." Consignment means that the gallery agrees to show your book, but it will only pay you your commission when the work is sold. The advantage to the gallery is that it can keep a full, ever-changing stock of new work without having to take any risk. Many times the galleries that carry book art are small and not well financed; it is advantageous to the community to keep them open, even if that means leaving work on consignment. The advantage to the artist is that if she is not well established, she has an easy place to show and sell her work. The disadvantage is that if the book doesn't sell, the artist may get back a worn-out copy that is unsalable. Determine a fair amount of time to leave the book on consignment. I don't recommend more than six months.

Exhibitions

Search art magazines for *call for entries* that accept book art. When you enter shows you will need slides. Gallery curators will rarely consider the actual book object. As a matter of principle, I try to avoid shows that charge entry (submission) fees. Even when you pay to enter the show, there is no guarantee your books will be accepted. Local galleries, community centers, or public libraries may also have listings for exhibits.

Often, people do not think of exhibitions as places to buy art, but only as places to view it. Keep a list of exhibitions in which you are included. A gallery may want a resumé before it will accept your books.

Other Ideas

Some indirect ways of getting yourself known may help sell your work. Teach a class, volunteer in a school, write for a grant, organize a project, organize a book fair at a community center, help with larger book fairs, volunteer with book arts organizations. You may get invited to participate in other exhibits and events once people get to know you. You may also get to know some other wonderful and enthusiastic book artists. See www.neverbook.com for links to related book arts sites.

CONCLUSION

I heard a story about a baker. He had made pies for years and years and they were perfect. One day he mistakenly left a thumb print in one of the piecrusts. That day he sold the pie with the thumb print first. Suddenly he was aware that people like to know that a human actually made the goods. Does the thumb print signify a mistake? Reassurance that no one is perfect? Reassurance that a person made the pie, that it wasn't made by machine? In the late 1800s the Industrial Revolution changed how people thought about the world. Eventually, the craftsperson was driven out of business by factories that could make the same item faster and cheaper. Now, at the beginning of the 21st century we are finding that we miss the look and feel of things made by hand; we are buying the irregular piecrust with the thumb print. The story is about all aspects of making things—in our case making book art.

Your books must be technically proficient to be taken seriously, but something of you must show; it must be apparent that you touched every piece included in your book. Maybe you decorated the paper, or painted the

Robbin Ami Silverberg: *titok*, 1996/98; detail of 27 4" boxes (photo by József Rosta)

Noises in the House, 1997; paper mâché boxes with rattles inside

cover, cut out shapes in the pages, or added tags, doors, or windows. An unusual structure shows that you thought about the content and that the theme of your book is echoed in it.

Handmade books often have special papers that have special sounds and smells. Work with different materials and find which ones you prefer. Do you like painting the pages? Drawing with watercolor pencils? Using photocopies or found objects? Cutting and pasting collages? Writing teachers talk about finding your own voice; you can find your own voice in your handmade books when you discover your favorite materials and use them in different ways again and again.

Your books will soon have an identity; only you could have made them. We often define ourselves by our stuff: what colors we like, the things we collect, the way we arrange pictures on a blank wall. Look in your desk drawer and you may find a collection: canceled stamps, dried flower petals, beads, or pens. What does this say about you and your relationship to the world? Create a book from your collection.

Choices, 2000; scroll with paste paper, dowel, particleboard (recycled linoleum block), ink bottles, acrylics; 10" x 8" x 6"

The more books you make, the better you get at both the art and the craft. Give yourself time to practice. Be flexible and willing to explore. As you explore, you will learn to make sturdy books that convey your unique vision. But don't stop there. Although you may never think you're done, show your work. Just as the thirteen contributors to this book were inspiration for me, your personal expression can become inspiration for others.

CONTRIBUTORS

Julie Chen is a book artist in Berkeley, California. She publishes work under the Flying Fish Press imprint and teaches book arts classes at Mills College. She also teaches workshops at various institutions around the country.

Sas Colby is an artist and teacher who works in Berkeley, California, and Taos, New Mexico.

Betsy Davids is an artist and writer who teaches writing and bookmaking at California College of Arts and Crafts in Oakland. She is a founder of the Pacific Center for the Book Arts.

Marie C. Dern is a teacher, book artist, former president of the Pacific Center for the Book Arts, and proprietor of Jungle Garden Press in Northern California.

Alisa Golden is the author of *Creating Handmade Books* (Sterling Publishing Co., Inc., 1998), former board member of the Pacific Center for the Book Arts, book artist, and printmaker working under the imprint never mind the press.

Alastair Johnston is the author of *Alphabets to Order: The Literature of Nineteenth-Century Typefounders' Specimens* (Oak Knoll Books/The British Library: 2000), editor of the Pacific Center for the Book Arts' journal *The Ampersand*, teacher, and letterpress printer of Poltroon Press.

Lisa Kokin is an artist who works with found materials. For her internationally exhibited book art and assemblages she has received numerous awards, including a California Arts Council Visual Arts Fellowship. She teaches art in nursing homes and homeless shelters in the San Francisco Bay area.

Catherine Michaelis is a book artist and letterpress printer in Vashon Island, Washington, working under the imprint May Day Press.

Katherine Ng is the director of the Letterpress Studio at the Armory Center for the Arts. She is a book artist, letterpress printer, and teacher in Southern California, working under the imprint Pressious Jade.

Coriander Reisbord is a conservation bookbinder, teacher, president of the Pacific Center for the Book Arts, and proprietor of Skeptical Press, in the San Francisco Bay area.

Anne Hicks Siberell is a writer and artist working in Hillsborough, California. Her commercially published books include *Whale in the Sky*, a PBS Reading Rainbow book. She is currently working on a children's book *Bravo! Brava! OPERA*, to be published by Oxford University Press.

Robbin Ami Silverberg is director of Dobbin Mill/Dobbin Books in New York. Her time is divided between making solo artist books, large paper installations, and artist book collaborations. She has both exhibited and taught extensively in the United States, Canada, South Africa, and Europe.

Val Simonetti is a book artist and letterpress printer in Richmond, California, working under the imprint Hand-in-Glove Press.

Anne Hayden Stevens (née Schwartzburg) is an painter and book artist living and working in Seattle. She teaches digital media and drawing at the University of Washington, in the Department of Architecture and School of Art.

For more about Betsy Davids, Sas Colby, Julie Chen, and Alisa Golden see the book *Speaking of Book Art: Interviews with British and American Book Artists,* by Cathy Courtney.

INDEX

Metric Conversion Chart

MM=Millemeters CM=Centimeters

Inches	MM	CM	Inches	CM
1/8	3	0.3	4	10.2
1/4	6	0.6	4½	11.4
3/8	10	1.0	5	12.7
1/2	13	1.3	6	15.2
5/8	16	1.6	7	17.8
3/4	19	1.9	8	20.3
7/8	22	2.2	9	22.9
1	25	2.5	10	25.4
1¼	32	3.2	11	27.9
1½	38	3.8	12	30.5
1¾	44	4.4	13	33.0
2	51	5.1	14	35.6
2½	64	6.4	15	38.1
3	76	7.6	16	40.6
3½	89	8.9		